PROFILES IN PATRIOTIC LEADERSHIP

By Greg Slavonic, Rear Admiral, U.S. Navy (Retired)

Contributors (alphabetically):

Brian T. Costello, Captain, U.S. Navy (Retired)
Kevin Elliot, Master Chief, U.S. Navy
Thomas F. Hall, former Assistant Secretary of Defense (Manpower & Reserve Affairs)
Steve Valley, Command Sergeant Major, U.S. Army Reserve
John Wagner, Major, U.S. Army Reserve
Donald J. Wetekam, Lieutenant General, USAF (Retired)
Rob Wray, Rear Admiral, U.S. Navy
James G. Zumwalt, Lieutenant Colonel, U.S. Marine Corps (Retired)

I0026625

FORTIS

A NON-FICTION IMPRINT FROM ADDUCENT

Adducent, Inc.

www.Adducent.Co

<u>Titles Distributed In</u>
North America
United Kingdom
Western Europe
South America
Australia

Profiles in Patriotic Leadership

By Greg Slavonic

ISBN 978-1-937592-17-2

Published by Adducent (under its Fortis non-fiction imprint)

Jacksonville, Florida

www.Adducent.Co

Published in the United States of America

TABLE OF CONTENTS

DEDICATION

This book is dedicated to the men and women who have served, who are serving and who will serve… and who proudly wear the cloth of our great Nation. They travel in harm's way all over the world to ensure we have the freedom we enjoy every day. Thank you!

ACKNOWLEDGMENTS

I would like to thank the following contributors to the book for sharing their insights and experiences with us:

Honorable Tom Hall, former Assistant Secretary of Defense (Manpower & Reserve Affairs) and retired Rear Admiral;

Lieutenant General Don Wetekam, U.S. Air Force (Retired) – Senior Vice President AAR;

Rear Admiral Robert Wray, U.S. Navy – President, Board of Inspection and Service (INSERV);

Captain Brian Costello, U.S. Navy (Retired) – former Commander, Strategic Communications Wing ONE and current President of Avalon Correctional Services;

Lieutenant Colonel Jim Zumwalt, U.S. Marine Corps (Retired) – author *"Bare Feet – Strong Will – Stories from the other side of Vietnam's Battlefields"* and author of – *"Living the Juche Lie / North Korea's Kim Dynasty"* and son of Admiral Elmo Zumwalt (Chief of Naval Operations);

Major John Wagner, U.S. Army Reserve – Iraqi war veteran and current spokesman at U.S. Central Command, Tampa, FL.;

Command Sergeant Major Steve Valley, USAR – currently CSM for the 205th Public Affairs Operations Center and author *"Inside the Fortress";* and,

Master Chief D. Kevin Elliott, U.S. Navy – currently Senior Enlisted Advisor for the Vice Chief of Information.

In addition, I would personally like to thank **Lieutenant Colonel Allen West,** U.S. Army (Retired), Congressman from the State of Florida and a combat veteran; for writing the foreword to this book.

Food for thought: 2012 will be the first presidential election since 1944 where neither candidate has served in the military. Coupled with the fact that only 22% of the members of Congress have served in the military—the lowest number since at least World War II—our country needs Lieutenant Colonel Allen West and more like him in Washington DC. Veterans like Congressman West display the type of "leadership" essential in Congress to ensure our nation remains safe and to ensure someone will always "have the backs" of our service members until they return home.

FOREWORD

Leadership is the difference between some of us falling, and all of us pulling through. The good leader is a person of courage, competence, commitment, conviction and character. A leader must possess impeccable integrity and ability that would carry them through any crisis, challenge or task successfully without being concerned about others. But for him or her, that's not enough. They hang back, take care of others who are getting weak or having trouble driving on. A leader helps others push through and find the strength they never knew they had. A strong leader is the reason that no one gets left behind. Good leadership is the cornerstone for any successful organization.

From the moment a recruit shows up at Basic Training, Marine Corps Boot Camp or Officer Candidate School, to the hardest parts of the Special Forces Q Course or Navy SEAL selection, the US military knows it needs to look for leaders. The ones who are strong enough and smart enough to make it through are valuable, but the ones who fall back and help others are the ones the hardship is really intended to find. These leaders are spotted in training, and their only reward is to have more work, more hardship and more responsibility laid on them. The ones who pull through these additional tasks and responsibilities are fast-tracked for leadership slots. They are tested and retested and developed throughout their career. They are the rock on which our fighting prowess stands. They are the reason that the American military can take on anyone in the world.

"Profiles in Patriotic Leadership" is a selected group of writings by respected leaders who share their experiences with the reader and what they feel are essential elements of leadership. Each story covers the broadest possible view of leadership and crystallizes it into essential models of success. All contributors to the book have demonstrated they can successfully lead in a "high stress", crisis environment which should make this book of extreme interest to anyone in business who wants to develop their leadership skills and lead others to achieve their individual or corporate goals within your organization.

Lieutenant Colonel Allen West, U.S. Army (Retired)
Congressman, United States House of Representatives
State of Florida
Committee on Armed Services

CHAPTER 1
THE BUCK STOPS WITH THE LEADER

"Men make history, and not the other way around. In periods where there is no leadership, society stands still. Progress occurs when courageous, skillful leaders seize the opportunity to change things for the better."

- Harry S. Truman

Greg Slavonic, Rear Admiral, U.S. Navy (Retired)

Profiles in Patriotic Leadership

Leadership is a word heard in the news every day. It has received much emphasis over the past four years due to, what some would say, is a failure of leadership by many in positions of authority within the government and corporate America.

Leadership is easily defined and interpreted. But there are different perspectives on how to be a leader and leading an organization. Today, as never before in our country's history, we need true leaders in every walk of life whether in corporations, as elected officials, in sports, and even in our military.

Leaders who come from a military career or who have previously served in the military have a unique understanding on what it takes to lead. And that translates easier than one would think into effective leadership in today's business and political environment. In the military, when a person is given the responsibility to lead, he or she does exactly that – they lead. Those serving under that leadership can trust and believe in what they say. Their word is their bond.

Today we live in a society where many often "misspeak". It is difficult for me to understand why it is so hard for those in positions of power, both in the public and private sector, to be honest and forthright with the individuals they are responsible to lead or govern. There appears to be more energy spent by them spinning or couching what they say rather than telling the truth. In the current climate, whether in politics or business, it is difficult today to take a leader at their word. What they've said in the past contradicts the present and that in turn twists and turns in what they say in the future. I can certainly understand an evolving policy that requires a reversal or change in position—but not explaining, not communicating their position, or outright misleading an individual, a group or nation is totally unacceptable.

An increasing number of our leaders are influenced and aided financially by special interest groups. This occurs in politics and board rooms across this country from small counties to large cities. Good leaders are expected to provide solid leadership for the best interest of the organization they have been hired by or elected to represent. But if that is counter to the interests of the select individuals or special interest groups then what do you think happens? Conflict of interest at worst and ineffectiveness to do what's right at best. Today we need leaders and leadership that does the right thing; people that do what is needed regardless of special interest.

True leaders, whether in the military or government, are rightfully held to higher standards by the public. They are expected to embody positive ethical standards and values while leading from the front and not comprising their integrity, character or ethics. I've observed leaders who are humble in their approach to their job and are successful with that style. I've also seen leaders who were charismatic and lead through the power of personality and have witnessed those who are more rigid in their leadership approach and they too are successful. Each of these approaches can be fair, objective and effective. Basically leadership comes down to individual characteristics that each successful person has developed over the course of their career. No matter the style, manner or approach that individual is expected to be a positive example to those they lead.

In the military a successful leader is selected for a particular position because they have the training, education, experience and have demonstrated the capacity to lead. Each must do exactly that – LEAD. Each must articulate a clear and concise vision, and their approach to achieve the mission. Those ideas and vision are critical to achieving organizational goals. A leader must also understand not everyone will share the vision or grasp the essence of the ideas but in a crisis he/she must lead and make decision without debate or discussion. The ability to effectively communicate to those he/she leads is essential in today's environment – the ability to cut through the chatter and tail-chasing discussions to come to grips with and execute a solution is even more important.

There needs to be a balance between effective communication and action. Frequently we see leaders (especially political) say one thing to get elected and once elected fail to fulfill their campaign platform. It is truly refreshing today to have elected leaders like Governors Scott Walker (Wisconsin), John Kasich (Ohio), Mitch Daniels (Indiana), Congressman, and former Lieutenant Colonel, Allen West (Florida), to name a few who truly understand the words commitment, integrity, and character. These words are closely associated with our military and should be associated within the business and political culture too.

The buck stops with the leader. A leader will gain respect of his followers when they understand and respect his/her position on an issue or situation. A leader must face reality. Reality starts with the person in charge. Leaders need to look at themselves in the mirror and recognize they are tasked with realizing the problem and having to develop a solution. Sometimes this will require quick action or a decision when operating in a crisis. Other times it occurs in a less demanding environment. Some say while recognition of reality is the crucial step before problems can be solved; attempting short-term fixes that address the symptoms of the crisis will only ensure the organization will wind up back in the same predicament. I disagree. Often times a 70 or 80 percent solution is required not 100% or a perfect one. Once a leader has determined the "way ahead" then they must explain the plan and then execute (lead).

Leaders create transformational change through having a vision and clearly sharing it with others. GEN (Ret) David Petraeus was one of the best at doing this in the military. I feel strongly, GEN Petraeus selection as Commander MultiNational Force–Iraq (MNF-I) was the key factor to a successful troop drawdown in Iraq. Some would say, if he were selected to lead sooner, U.S. success could have been accelerated and achieved two or three years earlier. With earlier success, the number of American lives lost could have been significantly less. GEN Petraeus knew the environment, the tribal culture, the people, and had the ability and persona to effectively communicate the way ahead and U.S./Coalition intent during the transition Iraq and the US.

Military leaders live and display a daily set of principles which are recognized by others. Character is developed at an early age and grows over time. Respected leaders "walk the walk and talk the talk". The character of the leader is consistent and is on display 24/7... not when it's convenient or to fit a particular situation. A person's reputation follows him/her throughout the balance of his/her career. Hence, I like to stress the importance of what I call reputation management. I had the good fortune to serve in the military for 34 years and I have always felt reputation management is essential in any environment. You should always be honest, forthright and ethical in your dealings with anyone—either in a business, personal or military setting. Maintaining an honest and upfront professional relationship with an individual or group is important. Communicating intent is critical to build positive relationships with subordinates or colleagues and cannot be over stated.

 In the workplace, if asking others to do something or make a sacrifice, you as a leader must first volunteer yourself. If there are sacrifices to be made – and there will be – then the leaders need to step up and make the greatest sacrifice themselves. Everyone is watching to see what you as a leader will do. Will you stay true to values? Will you bow to external pressures, or confront the crisis in a straight on? This is how you will be measured and evaluated.

There was a young Lieutenant Commander who worked for me during the First Gulf War. Our staff learned the mission to liberate Kuwait from Iraqi control would begin in a few days. I needed to dispatch a "Combat Correspondent Pool (CCP)" to embark on the USS *Saratoga* (CVA 60) operating in the Red Sea. (*CCPs were sent to various forward operating units within the theater of operation – whether Army, Air Force, Marines or Navy. During the early stages of the war, it was important for the journalists to be pre-positioned before operations commenced.*) I needed an escort for the CCP and this Lieutenant Commander was the right person to escort the media pool of twelve journalists. They departed from Dhahran (located in Saudi Arabia's Eastern Province) and traveled across Saudi Arabia to reach the *Saratoga*. They would capture stories which would provide the American public with firsthand accounts of brave Navy pilots before they launched and on their return. Unfortunately, not all returned the first days of the war. Once operations were well underway the CCP was directed back to Dhahran, so they could rotate with other journalists who were in theater to cover the war.

The young Lieutenant Commander prepared his group for their departure and return. They boarded the Navy C-2A Greyhound logistics aircraft and were launched from the *Saratoga*. In order to make the long transit from the Red Sea across Saudi Arabia to Dhahran a refueling stop was required at the Saudi Royal Air Force Base near Riyadh (the capital and largest city of Saudi Arabia). Once on the ground and while the plane was refueling suddenly air raid sirens sounded which meant radar had detected an incoming SCUD missile and the base was the potential target. (*Note: early in the war, SCUD attacks were a daily occurrence – sometimes two and three times a day. These rockets were launched from portable launchers and often were difficult to detect. Once launched, the targeting system employed by the Iraqi was not the most high tech. The U.S. deployed the Patriot defense system in theater to target and knock down these missiles. The Patriot system would hit the missile before striking the intended target and frequently the rocket was destroyed but would break apart, creating falling debris that at times covered a large area. In addition, since the Iraqi government threatened deploying chemical or biological agents on their warheads, the falling debris field was an even greater concern.*) Once the sirens sounded the Lieutenant Commander and journalists donned their gas masks and took cover in the bunkers near the runway. When the Lieutenant Commander got to the bunker there was a Saudi mother and her child already hunkered down inside. Sirens blaring, the mother was scared and crying. The lieutenant commander took off his mask and offered it to the mother and she said, "No, I want my daughter to wear it." So he put it on her daughter, cinched it up and waited. The sirens sounded for twenty minutes and the SCUD hit a few miles away. It was determined the warhead was conventional and did not contain a chemical or biological agent. This young naval officer did not actually save the life of the young child, but if the missile had a chemical or biological agent and struck nearby it could have made the difference in life or death of a child. His actions, no doubt, made a positive impact on those he was leading and one would think, on the Saudi mother, as well.

When you're in a leadership position you'll never know how you will react to a particular situation, so you should always be prepared. Leaders often have to make spilt-second decisions. I knew this individual for many years and his actions were not surprising because of the type of person he was. He stayed true to his values. (I believe this type of story, of our men and women in uniform, exercising true leadership, happens daily and goes unreported.)

An area of increasing concern, which I see every day, is when character and position come in conflict; when a leader's ego collides with the power of his position. Leaders who possess a large ego and are charged with leading an organization can find themselves at a personal crossroads. If the leader is unable to hold his/her ego in check then the power associated with the individuals position will lead to problems within the organization. Ego will lead them to believe they are above the rules that govern everyone else. Since they have achieved this high level of responsibility or prestige they feel a different set of rules and guidelines apply to them.

The military is held to a higher standard in the eyes of most Americans. And it holds itself to higher standards to deal with all manner of difficult and complex issues. Since 2010, the United States Navy has relieved dozens of commanding officers and in 2012 is on a pace to break 2003 record firings. The United States Navy does not hesitate to make a change at the top when allegations are brought against a person in a leadership position. Most terminations have been due to offenses of a sexual nature, alcohol and substance abuse, or other personal misconduct. Ego and power have certainly been elements in several of these firings which have led to a loss of confidence that these leaders can lead. These problems have shaken the senior ranks which has traditionally been the group which the Navy has taken pride in cultivating and promoting as its finest leaders.

As former Chief of Naval Operations Admiral Gary Roughead said, "The Navy was duty-bound to uphold strict behavioral standards, even when commanders are off-duty... does it really matter what a commanding officer does in their personal life?"

Admiral Roughead went on to say, "We believe it does, because it gets right to the issue of integrity and personal conduct and trust and the ability to enforce standard." The Navy is not the only military service plagued by poor decision-making in its upper ranks. The U.S. Army has disciplined or relieved senior leadership too. The command climate is critical to establishing a solid, well run, efficient operating unit or company. This can only be accomplished by top-down leadership. The leader must lead by example, day or night, as stated by Admiral Roughead.

Unfortunately the case is much different in the military. Firings in the corporate world rarely garner the level of media interest as those in the military unless it is a big-name CEO. Martha Stewart was forced to resign from her media empire and spend time in jail after being convicted of lying about an illegal stock trade she made in another company's shares but she returned to an almost "celebrity-like" profile and is certainly still worth many millions of dollars. Best Buy CEO Brian Dunn resigned after the Board of Directors launched an investigation into his personal conduct but he will receive his lucrative severance package. Mark Hurd, CEO of Hewlett-Packard falsified reports to disguise expense reports for meals and travel and received $30 million on his way out the door, and less than a month later joined his competition Oracle as Co-president. The consequences of their actions did not impede their financial benefit and in some cases their careers.

In the military once relieved of command, one's career is over. In the military a person's character, integrity and ethical behavior matters because those traits are the very essence of a military tradition that makes the military the greatest organization if not in the world, then certainly in the United States. When these traits are compromised, the leader is no longer able to lead and command because of loss of respect.

I was selected for flag rank in 2000 and was invited to attend the flag officer orientation conference. The conference brought together all the newly selected flag officers to receive briefings on several different issues. One of the briefings was on ethical behavior. The 3-star admiral opened this presentation by saying, "Look to your left and look to your right... in less than two years one of these individuals will no longer be serving in the US Navy." Needless to say, that comment captured everyone's attention. His presentation captured the heart and meaning of ethical behavior and making the right decision when you find yourself in a situation where it was clear what the right course of action was.

We were told to ask ourselves the following question, "What if our decision appeared on the front page of the New York Times – would we be able to stand the scrutiny?" The pressures of making "the wrong decision" and becoming a statistic are published every day in the New York Times. There are too many admirals and senior officers who can't pass muster that are being relieved and that is a sad commentary on our command environment today. But the point to make here is that the military does purge poor leaders—there is accountability and that is an important lesson that those in leadership positions in government and in business need to learn.

When you become a leader in a highly visible position you must always be aware of public perception. A case in point concerns a fellow flag officer when he was searching for a flag aide replacement. A flag aide's responsibility requires long periods of traveled with his or her boss, long hours together reviewing paperwork, preparing briefings, speeches, planning, etc. The list goes on. Long days working together are not unusual and come with the job. This flag officer's decision came down to two highly qualified, professional officers: one male and the other female. He decided it was in his best interests, his family, and the US Navy to select the male as the flag aide. He was not worried about himself or the female candidate but given the amount of time they would be spending together over the next year he was concerned about the perception on the part of the public or even within the military community. He wanted to remove any hint of impropriety by external audiences which could affect his ability to lead the people he would be in contact with on a daily basis. Perception is reality. Although, perception can be skewed by many factors we are often evaluated – right or wrong – by the perception of others. Being a Navy flag officer brings a great deal of power which can have an impact on the individuals within the command and those working for him or her.

This is just as true in the corporate and political world. The impact power (its misuse and proper use) has, for bad and good, every day is dramatic; especially in the political arena from its epicenter, our nation's capital in Washington, DC, down to local political circles.

Youth today need role models. They need leaders they respect, that have character, and integrity. Where do most young people look for their role models? I believe many gravitate to the world of sports. While many may disagree, I have seen far too often the impact athletes have on young people. High school baseball players chew or dip tobacco because this is what college and big league players do. High school football players take growth enhancement supplements to get bigger and stronger because this is what college and professional players do. And the list goes on.

Then you have the moral issues.

Tiger Woods' behavior and personal indiscretions are well documented by thousands of headlines, photographs, interviews, paparazzi frenzy, "he said and she said", and "film at eleven." While he lost millions of dollars in sponsorships, the negative affect he had on our youth is incalculable.

Woods rose to be the best of best in a sport dominated by white male athletes—he was a high-profile role model in a sport that focuses on the merits and skill of the individual. And failed to live up to what is expected of such a role model when he made several poor choices

14

that were put on full display for the world to see. Will Woods' position as a role model change the young people's, that idolized him, attitude about how to live their lives? Woods' situation goes back to my earlier point: when ego and power collide... problems occur.

Of course, drugs have no place in the world today, especially in the world of sports, but I'm told by those in the medical field performance enhancing drugs are in all areas of sports. There are many stories of drug usage in cycling, track and field, football, and I'm even told in golf. Baseball has been in the news often the past several years especially and two names in the headlines are Roger Clemens and Barry Bonds. They are both trying to resolve their problems through the legal system being accused of using performance enhancing drugs during their baseball careers. Again, these men (and other sports figures) purport to be "role models/leaders" for our youth.

There is hope and there are stories of individuals making the right decision, the tough decision every day. The decisions which have to be made by individuals put in positions of great responsibility. The decisions must be made for the greater good of the organization.

Here is a story from the sports world. You probably don't recognize the name of Jeff Long unless you are a follower, supporter or graduate of the University of Arkansas. Long is the Vice Chancellor and Director of Athletics at the University of Arkansas. Long had to fire

Bobby Petrino, the head football coach who had hired his own mistress. Petrino intentionally mislead Long about his relationship with her and her presence as a rider on a motorcycle driven by Petrino involved in a motorcycle accident.

Petrino turned a losing team into a winning team in only two years and took the team to a major bowl game. In the world of college football winning equals big money to the athletic department. Winning on the football field is what alumni expect. Alumni contribute money to winning teams to ensure they continue to win. But success should never shield a purported leader from their indiscretions or their errors in judgment even at a personal level such as Petrino's. Long could not tolerate it and nor should any organization (military, public, private or educational) who bear a public trust to represent principles and ideals that guide and shape our young.

Long put his stamp on Razorback athletics through an innovative reorganization and streamlining the administration. His vision and goal was for the University of Arkansas to become a model within NCAA athletics. Along with creating a new internal structure, Long has Arkansas on the path to not only maintain its place as one of the nation's top programs, but to elevate its status by enhancing the Razorback program to an even higher level of achievement and respect.

When reviewing Long's resume, how often can you recall one that states the following, "his guiding principles of <u>integrity,</u> winning, community service and the promotion of a quality experience for each of the more than 450 Razorback student-athletes..." I must admit I've reviewed many resumes and NEVER did the word "integrity" appear in an individual narrative when outlining a person's goals and accomplishments or vision.

With leaders that make integrity, character and accountability part of their personal philosophy there is hope, not only in the world of sports, but in many walks of life.

* * *

I'll close the chapter with this—and I think it perhaps is the core of what makes a person a good leader – what makes a good leader great and what makes a great leader achieve what some feel is impossible.

In former General's Colin Powell's recently published book, *It Worked for Me*, he shares an interesting leadership story which I feel bears repeating. When serving as Secretary of State, Powell decided to slip away from his elegant office and sneak down to the garage to visit with employees. Of course this group of workers, consisting of immigrants and minorities making minimum wage, had never seen a Cabinet Secretary wandering around the garage before and they asked the obvious question, "Are you lost and do you need directions back your office?" Powell replied, "No, I just wanted to chat."

He shared this experience at the next staff meeting with his senior leaders; Powell telling them, "You can never err by treating everyone in the building with respect, thoughtfulness, and a kind word."

Powell's take away from this experience was that every individual in an organization has value and "wants that value to be recognized". Every employee you're entrusted to lead and are responsible for needs appreciation and reinforcement. A leader must take care of every member of this team. Powell goes on to articulate, "I believe that if you develop a reputation of kindness, even the most unpleasant decisions will go down easier... as the old saying goes... to the world, you may be one person, but to one person you may be the world."

That "old saying" is a perspective that puts everything in context and squarely defines how important a leader's responsibility is to those they lead.

Greg Slavonic

BIOGRAPHY

Rear Admiral Greg Slavonic, U.S. Navy (Retired) a native of Great Bend, Kansas, and raised in Oklahoma City, most recently served as the U.S. Navy's Deputy to the Chief of Information in Washington, D.C., and Director of Public Affairs (Reserve) from June 2001 to 2005. In this duel role, he served as principal advisor to the Chief of Information having responsibility for formulating strategic communications counsel to the leadership of the Department of the Navy. As part of his duties, he established and maintained professional working relationships and liaison with Navy Secretariat officers, other Department of Defense commands and activities within the Pentagon and in the Washington Capitol Region. In addition, he was responsible for the training and

Profiles in Patriotic Leadership

readiness of more than 500 public affairs reservists assigned to 26 different units across the United States.

In June 2004, Rear Admiral Slavonic deployed to support Operation Enduring Freedom II, Baghdad, Iraq. Assigned to the Multinational Force-Iraq (MNF-I) staff; he served as the senior strategic communications and public affairs officer for Commanding General for MNF-I, and directed daily operations at the combat Combined Press Information Center (CPIC). He worked closely with the White House and served as senior on-scene coordinator for the first court appearance at Camp Victory (Baghdad) by Saddam Hussein, plus eleven other high value detainees including Ali Hassan al Majid al-Tikriti ("Chemical Ali"). He led a crisis action team to the Babylon (Iraq) archaeological site numerous times to gather facts to defuse negative media coverage of MNF-I operations at the historical site. He was the first U.S. Navy flag officer assigned to MNF-I and the highest-ranking public affairs officer in Iraq.

In November 1990, Rear Admiral Slavonic deployed to Operations *Desert Shield* and *Desert Storm*. He was assigned to the staff of General H. Norman Schwarzkopf at U.S. Central Command and served at the Joint Information Bureau in Dhahran, Saudi Arabia. During his tour in the Arabian Gulf Theater, Rear Admiral Slavonic served as a Chief of Navy News desk and senior Combat Media Escort officer. This included escorting four Combat Correspondent Pools (CCP). Of note, he was aboard USS *Curts* (FFG-38) to document the processing and interrogation of more than 40 Iraqi prisoners. Then was aboard the amphibious assault ship USS *Tripoli* (LPH-10) when she struck an Iraqi underwater tethered mine causing extensive damage, flooding, and nearly sinking the ship.

Greg Slavonic

After graduating with a Bachelor of Science degree from Oklahoma State University, Rear Admiral Slavonic enlisted in the Navy. After completing boot camp and Signalman "A" school, he received orders to the aircraft carrier USS *Constellation* (CVA-64) and completed two western Pacific deployments in support of combat operations in Vietnam. Rear Admiral Slavonic affiliated with the Navy Reserve and received a commission as a restricted line officer in public affairs. In 1976, he earned a Master's degree from the University of Central Oklahoma. His military decorations include Bronze Star Medal (two awards), Legion of Merit Medal, Presidential Unit Commendation, Combat Action Ribbon and numerous other campaign and service awards.

Rear Admiral Slavonic served four commanding officer tours, staff public affairs officer for the Commander, Readiness Command Eleven and was a key member of the commissioning committee for the nuclear-powered, fast-attack submarine USS *Oklahoma City* (SSN 723). His civilian employment includes over 35 years in media and management as account executive with The (Daily) Oklahoma; advertising director for The Journal Record; general manager for the Oklahoma Gazette and senior account executive with KFOR-TV (NBC affiliate.) He is currently the Principal Leader, Strategic Communications & Public Affairs for CSC (formerly Computer Sciences Corporation); a Washington D.C. based Defense Company and President, FlagBridge Strategic Communications, LLC.

Rear Admiral Slavonic has served on numerous boards and held many key leadership positions including co-chair and the lead effort to raise $1.1 million dollars for building a USS *Oklahoma* Memorial at Pearl Harbor. He was chair of the Oklahoma War on Terror Memorial; chair for the selection committee for the Jim Thorpe Award (Outstanding Defensive Back); minority partner for

21

Profiles in Patriotic Leadership

the Oklahoma City Cavalry professional basketball team, has received the "Distinguished Former Student" Award presented by the University of Central Oklahoma and "Distinguished Alumni" Award from Bishop McGuinness High School. He currently serves on the Board of Directors for Avalon Correctional Services, Inc., and Mount St. Mary's High School.

He is a former adjunct professor in the Department of Journalism & Broadcasting at University of Central Oklahoma and taught Leadership Development in the Meinders School of Business at Oklahoma City University. He is the author of *Leadership In Action | Principles Forged in the Crucible of Military Service Can Lead Corporate America Back to the Top* and co-authored the book – *Jim Thorpe Award – The First 20 Years.*

CHAPTER 2
STRIVING FOR GREATNESSS

"Honesty is the first chapter in the book of wisdom."

- Thomas Jefferson

Captain Brian Costello, U.S. Navy (Retired)

Every outstanding leader I have worked for, worked with or learned from over the years had this one thing in common: they were all striving for greatness. The methods they used to get there were numerous and varied, but this was the connecting thread. I've been fortunate to have witnessed leadership at its finest over the course of my career and my time at the U.S. Naval Academy and have been truly blessed to have some of that wisdom imparted to me. Before I talk about some of that, let me go back even further for an example of true leadership.

Growing up in northern New Jersey I had a pretty easy childhood. Year round sports kept me busy along with school and numerous other activities. As the fourth of six children in my family, I quickly developed into a fairly independent kid. My parents raised me right... instilling the necessary understanding of right and wrong and the importance of integrity. They also set an excellent example in the way they lived their lives and never compromised when it came down to "the right thing to do."

So I was lucky to have parents who set me on the right course, but it doesn't have to be your parents. When I got to High School I was very involved with varsity athletics and it was our football coach who set the next example for me. Our football coach was a man named Jack Jones. I don't think he stood more than 5 ft. 6 in. but he was a fierce competitor and he never settled for "good enough". If we did something wrong, we did it again and again. In addition to this attitude of never settling for anything less than great, Jack Jones understood how motivation and greatness were intertwined. He knew that what might motivate me might not motivate our quarterback or a defensive lineman and he used this knowledge to get us all to perform as a team at a level that was above our individual capabilities. Countless players who were coached by Jack Jones went on to play Division I football in college and two from my time there went on to the NFL. I believe that much of that success can be attributed to his leadership and his ability to motivate us to greatness.

This is what being a leader is all about; motivating others to perform a job or a mission or an assignment that they wouldn't ordinarily be inclined to perform and to do it at a level that is above and beyond normal expectations. So how did my high school football coach do this? Well, I believe it was due to the fact that he really got to know us and came to understand each of us individually—what made us tick and what our capabilities were. I like to think that this has been one of my strengths as a leader. I have always attempted to know the sailors, officers, men and women that I've been with and then create a vision and goal for all of us. Striving toward this goal, toward greatness, then becomes a team sport, where we're all in it together and we all share in the success of the team.

One of the difficulties in writing about greatness and great leaders is that it is not easily understood why we view one leader as great and another as just "so-so". And there is a third category of "poor" that we all have seen at one time or another. (By the way, we can learn just as much from a poor leader as we can from a great leader!) The problem is defining this greatness. I know it when I see it so let me talk about a few great ones I've come across.

When I was a midshipman at the Naval Academy, I had the honor to be led by a true American hero, Vice Admiral William Lawrence, Superintendent. Admiral Lawrence, a Commander at the time, was the Commanding Officer of VF-143 flying F-4 Phantoms off the USS Constellation in 1967 when he was forced to eject over Vietnam. He was captured and held for the next six years as a POW. As a senior officer POW he withstood an incredible amount of torture in the POW camp but he overcame this adversity and, in many ways, became stronger and better for the experience. He became well known for his ability to know everyone's name in camp, for his resistance to his captors, and for developing codes tapped on walls for communication among his fellow prisoners. Like I said a true American hero. He was a three sport star at the Naval Academy, graduated at the top of his class; he was the Brigade Commander and Class President. I ended up being one of the lucky ones as he came back to USNA as Superintendent for his last tour of duty. The impact he had on me and the thousands of other midshipmen he led was enormous. He never passed up the opportunity to offer a word of encouragement when he would see you on the academy grounds, "the yard" as it commonly called. He always had time and always carried his amazing background with grace and humility. He was a great leader. We knew it at the time and we aspired to be like him. There have been a few people in my life that I've been in awe of and Admiral Lawrence was the first.

The true backbone of the Navy are the Chief Petty Officers who make it run and I've seen some of the truest, most natural leaders among the CPO ranks. We would expect our Navy Chiefs to be leaders of the junior enlisted sailors and they do this without fail. They consistently turn 18 and 19 year-olds into motivated, trained experts in a wide variety of highly skilled fields. This is truly remarkable. What is even more remarkable is their ability to "lead" the officers who rank above them in the chain of command. It is widely understood that a Navy Chief is responsible for helping to teach and train officers. After all a Chief might have 20 or 25 years of experience under his belt where a junior officer might have only 2 or 3. Sharing this experience with the less experienced officers makes perfect sense. In my experience, the talented Chiefs become the leaders. The officers feel like they're in charge but many of their decisions are shaped by the guidance of the Chief Petty Officers.

I saw this over and over again as a pilot on EC-130 and E-6 aircraft. Both planes are crewed by pilots, navigators, and flight engineers and carry mission crewmembers performing essential communications tasks and equipment repairs. It is a highly complex and demanding mission environment and we have developed a "zero-defect" mentality. We must operate the aircraft safely. Obviously there are no second chances with aircraft safety. Also, we must perform our communications mission correctly, the first time, every time. In a real world scenario, there are no second chances for that either. The enlisted crewmembers I had the privilege to fly with performed their jobs flawlessly and never gave less than a full, 100 percent effort. As an Aircraft Commander and Mission Commander, I constantly relied on the leadership of our enlisted Flight Engineers and Communications Supervisors to ensure we were safe and to ensure we were successful with our mission requirements.

There are too many to name here but the common thread among all these great leaders was devotion to duty, calmness under pressure, and unwavering integrity and honesty. An extremely important lesson on leadership was taught to me early in my first squadron tour. Treat others with respect regardless of their rank or status. This is really pretty simple. In fact, it is the golden rule and its roots lie in the Bible... do unto others as you would have them do unto you. One Lieutenant Commander, single-handedly, showed through example how people should be treated with trust and respect up and down the chain of command. It was a powerful lesson that has stayed with me for all these years.

Another import leadership lesson was learned when I had the opportunity to serve on the staff of Vice Admiral Mike Bowman, Naval Air Forces Pacific Fleet. Admiral Bowman – truly cared about his sailors and cared for his sailors. He would gladly spend hours talking with sailors and I believe he felt that was more important than just about anything else he needed to do. He, more than just about anyone else I've worked with over the years possessed a true empathy for those that worked for him. He would celebrate their successes and would feel the pain of their failures. This is a trait that I have always tried to emulate though I'm sure could never come close to Admiral Bowman on this one.

When I received orders to Bahrain, to work as the Director of Plans and Policy on the staff of the U.S. Navy's Fifth Fleet, I felt like I was in a new world, the pace was relentless and I was asked to perform a job I really wasn't prepared to do. Vice Admiral Dave Nichols welcomed me aboard his staff and told me not to be afraid to step outside my comfort zone. I was going be meeting with Navy and Coast Guard leadership from 15 countries in the region, I was going to be briefing Carrier Strike Group Commanders as they entered the Arabian Gulf. These and other responsibilities demanded that I step up and perform. His advice was timely and right on target and it set me up for success in this position over the next year. Later, during his farewell speech to all of his staff members, he spoke of stepping out of your comfort zone again. He likened it to breaking through the scar tissue in his shoulder that hindered his arm movement after surgery. When he finally broke through that scar tissue it hurt a little but then he had his full range of motion back. He said that stepping outside you comfort zone is similar. A little scary at first but once you take that first step; a whole new world opens up to you. This advice has helped me over and over again during my career both in the military and now in the civilian business world.

So, how about a moment to mention some of the characteristics I've seen in "not so great" leaders. I think it is interesting that a poor leader can still get the job done, but the difference is that subordinates are not happy; they're not engaged and haven't taken ownership of the process or the mission. They are not willing to go the extra mile. This can be caused by a number of different things but, primarily, my experience has been that heavy-handed, overly authoritative leadership styles will sap the strength out of a unit or organization. Leaders who listen, who aren't afraid to involve subordinates in decisions, who recognize the talents of their team, and who create that team in the first place, these are leaders who have people that will consistently go the extra mile, "above and beyond the call of duty." I saw a commander once say to a young lieutenant, "I don't care if you're right, we doing this my way anyway." That lieutenant is not ever going to part of the team and others who saw or heard about this exchange will have a hard time being part of the team as well.

It's difficult to reflect on leadership and greatness without taking a moment to offer a tribute to the men and women, the sailors with whom I've have the opportunity to work with during my 26-year Navy career. I believe I've learned more from them than they have from me over the years. From the time I was an

Ensign till the day I retired as a Captain, I had a U.S. Navy Chief Petty Officer teaching me what I needed to know to do my job. These many, many Chiefs showed me what it means to take care of sailors and really care about those sailors. I am deeply indebted to so many individuals throughout the Navy's enlisted ranks who were constantly able to overcome adversity, who worked tirelessly in harsh conditions and who always got the job done because it had to get done. They consistently displayed a love of country and willingness to serve that is harder and harder to come by, and they never wavered from the overarching mission of the protection of our nation's freedoms and the preservation of our way of life.

So what is the common theme here? I believe there are many but, let me try to boil it down to a handful of common traits possessed by the great leaders I have seen in action. The first is empathy. I feel very strongly that you must be able to put yourself in someone else's shoes before you can lead them. I think great leaders have a keen understanding of the needs of those working for them. I often hear people say that a good leader will take care of his/her people. I agree but I would take that one step further and say that a great leader must genuinely *care* for those working for him/her.

This may be a subtle difference but I think it is an important distinction. Great leaders are all strong motivators. They understand that different people are motivated by different needs and they fit their message and vision to address those needs. Great leaders demand that no one settles for good enough. Settling for good enough ensures that the outcome will not be great. I have seen that a good sense of humor is often used to set a tone and keep people engaged. Nothing makes a leader more approachable than a little self-deprecating humor... and great leaders want to be approachable.

Without fail, I feel that unyielding integrity is essential for great leaders. If you forfeit your integrity you have also forfeited your ability to lead. Finally, I would offer that letting others speak and give ideas, and be willing to utilize those ideas is important for all leaders and empowering a subordinate in this way can often lead to tremendous results. Every great leader I have seen is always striving for greatness.

Greg Slavonic

BIOGRAPHY

Captain Costello is a native of New Jersey and received his Bachelor of Science degree in Operations Research and was commissioned in 1983 from the United States Naval Academy. He has over 25 years of leadership and management experience with extensive knowledge in command, control and communications.

He earned his pilot wings in 1985 and reported to Fleet Air Reconnaissance Squadron Four (VQ-4) in Patuxent River, Md., for his first TACAMO tour flying the EC-130. During this tour, he was designated as a Mission Commander and Instructor Pilot, and held the position of Pilot NATOPS Evaluator.

In 1989, Captain Costello was assigned to Training Squadron Six (VT-6) at Naval Air Station Whiting Field, Fla. In addition to his

Profiles in Patriotic Leadership

duties as Instructor Pilot in the T-34 aircraft, he held numerous other positions with the squadron, including CAT II Standardization Officer, Flight Officer and Operations Officer.

He returned to VQ-4 in 1992, now at Tinker AFB, Okla., where he qualified as an E-6 Aircraft Commander and Mission Commander. He was transferred to Strategic Communications Wing One (SCW-1) in 1994 and served as the Wing Maintenance Officer.

From 1995 to 1997, Captain Costello served as the Maintenance Officer for the Ironmen of Fleet Air Reconnaissance Squadron Three (VQ-3). During this time, he also re-qualified as an E-6 Mission Commander and Instructor Pilot.

Captain Costello was the E-6 Class Desk Officer on the staff of the Commander, Naval Air Force, U.S. Pacific Fleet in San Diego, during which time he was selected for Aviation Command. He reported back to VQ-3 for his tour as Executive Officer and Commanding Officer. During his command tour, the Ironmen were awarded the Battle E, the Safety S, and the Maintenance Excellence awards.

After his command tour, Captain Costello served as the CSCW-1 Deputy for Operations and Plans, then in March 2005, he reported to US Navy Fifth Fleet in Bahrain, where he served as the Plans, Policy and Political-Military Officer (N5) on the staff of US Naval Forces Central Command, in support of Operations Iraqi Freedom, Enduring Freedom and the Global War on Terrorism.

He returned to SCW-1 as Deputy Wing Commander in March 2006 and then assumed the Wing Commander assignment in July 2007. In this assignment he was responsible for the management of over 1,600 military and civilian personnel, a $120 million operating

Greg Slavonic

budget, and $3.8 billion in assets. He was also responsible for maintaining a Lean/Six Sigma based process improvement program that focused on cost avoidance, theory, and best practices.

His awards include; the Legion of Merit, Defense Meritorious Service Medal, two Meritorious Service Medals, three Navy and Marine Corps Commendation Medals, two Navy and Marine Corps Achievement Medals and various other personal and unit awards.

In August 2009 he became the President and Chief Operating Officer for Avalon Correctional Services where he is responsible for the Operations, Training, and Maintenance of 10 facilities in 3 states providing private community corrections and alternative correctional programming.

CHAPTER 3
AN EXAMPLE
WORTHY OF TRUST

"A leader leads by example, whether he intends to or not."

- Author Unknown

MCCM D. Kevin Elliott, U.S. Navy

There is no other rank in the military like that of a Navy Chief Petty Officer. In other branches of the armed forces when you are promoted to the senior enlisted rank of E-7 there is little or no fanfare or celebration. However, a Chief candidate isn't promoted solely on a written exam score; they must pass the exam and then be selected by a board of Master Chiefs and Commissioned Officers. They are then appointed by the Bureau of Naval Personnel and join the ranks of the Chief Petty Officers where they shed their former uniform and are initiated into a new world of responsibility and leadership.

Other uniformed services have equivalent pay grades (E-7 through E-9), but the Navy is unique in that it confers much more authority and responsibility on the Chief while demanding greater performance and results. It is a leadership role like none other in the world.

Leadership Defined

U.S. Navy War Instructions from 1944 define leadership as, "The art of inspiring, guiding and directing bodies of men so that they ardently desire to do what the leader wishes." In Management of Organizational Behavior: Utilizing Human Resources, leadership is defined as, "The process of influencing the activities of an individual or a group of individuals in efforts toward goal achievement in a given situation." In the Navy leaders set the course, but Navy leaders are different from the civilian world in that the course they set may send their sailors into harm's way.

At its core leadership is a relationship involving interaction between a leader and followers. The success of that interaction is the measure of a leader. Leaders create goals and the strategies needed to meet them.

They must motivate, inspire, and energize their sailors to overcome obstacles in order to align themselves with the course set by the leader. Before a leader can align their sailors with that course they must first ensure their own values are in alignment with those of the Navy.

In October 1992, the CNO Executive Steering Committee adopted the Core Values of "Honor, Courage and Commitment." The origins of these values are found in the oath of enlistment: "I will bear true faith and allegiance..." refers to honor. We must live and act in the highest ethical manner at all times, have an uncompromising code of integrity, take responsibility for our actions, and realize it is a privilege to serve our fellow Americans. "I will support and defend..." refers to courage. We must meet the demands of our chosen profession while adhering to a higher standard of personal conduct. We must ensure our nations resources entrusted to us are used honestly and carefully, and have the moral and mental strength to do what is right even in the face of adversity. "I will obey the orders..." refers to commitment. We must be committed to the chain of command, care for the well-being of our people, exhibit the highest degree of moral character, and work together as a team to ensure mission success.

Leaders must demonstrate personal integrity, require ethical behavior from their followers, and hold people accountable for unethical behavior. But first they must set an example. A Navy Chief Petty Officer is the standard by which all other sailors are measured. Not only are they technical experts, they are considered the backbone of the Navy.

By living a life based on honor, courage, and commitment, a leader will set a positive example worthy of trust. Trust is the first step toward aligning your people in the same direction and getting them to understand your vision.

Leaders Set the Tone

Leaders get out and walk around; they don't stay hidden in their office. Don't be a Ghost in the Machine. Get out and show your face. It makes you more approachable because people see you more as a team member. It's also important that your people know who is making the decisions as opposed to some mysterious person no one ever sees. Do something so that people recognize you are communicating your vision and goals.

I view leadership as an upside down pyramid. I work for my people. I owe them good leadership. Effective leaders tailor their style to the organization in order to ensure success. They must also adapt to the situation, beginning with an understanding of their people.

We must care for our people as we care for our own children. I gain great satisfaction when my own son is successful. In fact, I gain even more satisfaction than I do from my own accomplishments. There is no other feeling like it. The opposite is also true. When they fail, the leader fails. Each leader shares in their followers successes but also bears the weight of their failures. You have to work to keep and grow your people. Communicate with them. Don't wait for them to call you; call them. Offer education and leadership classes. Show concern for their welfare and be ready to use tough love.

A great leader practices personalized yet intrusive leadership. You must get to know your people. Learn their hobbies, interests, concerns, what they do on and off duty. Find out what makes them tick. When I was a young Chief Petty Officer there was an incident at a local Navy base. A young female sailor had left her baby locked up in her car on a hot summer day in Virginia and the baby died. In the investigation the sailor said she didn't have money to pay for a baby sitter. I wondered where her Chief was. If the Chief had been more intrusive in that young sailor's life and taken the time to get to know her, maybe her baby would be alive today.

I once encountered an admiral in my chain of command on three separate occasions. Out of those three times he said exactly two words to me. On another occasion I was attending a class with probably 50 other sailors and an admiral spoke to us, but before that he took the time to go around the room and spend some time with each sailor. He shook my hand, asked where I was from, asked about my family and just made small talk. I'm sure he spent less than 60 seconds with me but the impression he made will stick with me forever.

An intrusive leader will get to know their people. They will communicate standards and expectations of behavior. If they provide sound leadership, tools for success, established goals and a productive work environment their sailors will feel more connected, know they are contributing to the mission and will be more successful and less likely to go astray.

A Leader Without a Team is Nothing

It takes a team to succeed and a leader must develop a team that is accountable, capable and motivated. I view my sailors like the rungs of a ladder. In order for a ladder to work properly, all the rungs must be in place and the bottom rung is just as important as the top rung. That young sailor working in the galley or scrubbing the deck is just as important as the captain on the bridge. We are all in the same boat and we all benefit or suffer together. For a mission to succeed the team must thoroughly understand the goal and believe that success depends on their ability to work together effectively. Without a team, the leader is nothing.

The Navy is looking for leaders and you should seek out opportunities to lead. Don't be afraid to lead when your chance comes. I left on my annual training two days after being selected as a Chief so I was three weeks late to the initiation process. On my first day back I was standing in formation at Chiefs Initiation when the

Master Chief asked for someone to come up front and read the plan of the day. My fellow Chief selects had been at this for three weeks but no one moved. I gave it a few seconds and decided what the hell, I was a Navy Journalist and if nothing else, I knew how to read. So I took one step back, turned smartly and marched up front. I could hear a low murmur from the crowd as they watched the "new guy" step up. I was immediately surrounded by Chiefs who started yelling in my ears and applying pressure to see if I would flinch. But I stood my ground. I instinctively knew they were just trying to see what kind of a leader I was. I learned my first lesson that day. Show them who you are. Don't be afraid to be the leader. A Chief walked up to me afterwards and privately told me how proud everyone was to see me step up so soon. I went on to learn many lessons from that great group of Chiefs, Senior Chiefs and Master Chiefs. I know the lessons they imparted have helped me become the leader I am today and I am eternally grateful.

Make a Decision

Good leadership requires good decision making. I strive to make decisions based on the higher truth of Honor, Courage and Commitment. It's not possible to make a good unethical decision and you can't make a good decision that is contrary to the Navy's core values. I categorize decisions as either strategic or tactical. A strategic decision is long term with sufficient time to collect data and toss around ideas. Tactical decisions are short term where time is critical. Either way I try not to make a snap decision if I can keep from it. I like to weigh the risk or consequences of my decisions. That doesn't mean I never have to make a quick decision. At those times you have to rely on what some people call your intuition and others call a gut check. I call it that little voice in the back of my head. I've learned to trust that voice over the years and whenever I ignore that voice, I get in trouble.

Sailors are taught four styles of decision making; authoritative, consultative, facilitative and delegative. Authoritative means I'll decide. Consultative means let's talk then I'll decide. Facilitative means let's talk and then we'll decide together. Delegative means you decide. A good leader must adapt their decision making style to the situation.

Communication Goes Both Ways

The chain of command goes both ways and so does communication. The key to good decision making is good communication. You need to pass the correct information up and down the chain of command. Leaders spend more time communicating than probably any other single activity. If that leader doesn't communicate in a way people understand, their mission will probably fail.

There are four basic types of communication: reading, writing, speaking and listening. A successful leader needs to be good at all four, especially the listening part.

There is a difference between speaking and communicating. A leader communicates the mission; they don't just tell people their problems. Leaders need answers. I'm always happy to be a sounding board, but at the end of the day I need a solution, idea or recommendation. You can't just complain. But the leader also has to create an atmosphere of trust and responsibility so that everyone can communicate their concerns without fear of retribution.

Attention to Detail

My Chief at boot camp taught me about attention to detail and how it starts with your uniform. You can tell a lot about a sailor by how they wear their uniform. Is their collar insignia in the proper place, their ribbons in the correct order, their gig line straight? This is attention to detail and missing one small detail can sink a ship. Leave a valve open or fail to inform your chain of command about a mishap and you lose the ship. Leaders are always being watched. They wear their uniform correctly and with pride. A Chief Petty Officer is a role model and has the potential to influence every sailor in the Navy in either a positive or negative way.

It seems popular among leaders to say you have an "open door policy." You want people to know you are approachable but you have to be careful not to give the impression that the chain of command doesn't matter. If I have a First Class Petty Officer coming straight to me, my first question is always, "Did you speak with your Chief first?" Then my second question is for the Chief and why they aren't teaching the importance of chain of command.

Military members are held to a higher standard. Whenever you read a newspaper story about someone who did something wrong, it doesn't matter if it had something to do with the military or not. If you are in the Navy, the media says, "John Smith, a U.S. Navy sailor..." Be mindful of your obligations to the citizens of our great country and if you are in the Navy, you are in the Navy 24/7. It's like back in grade school when your class would go on a field trip the principal would always remind you that you represent the school. Act accordingly.

I always tell my son, "Success is its own reward." When you find a successful organization, you will find a successful leader. You will find an organization with established clearly defined goals and subordinates who believe the goals are important and attainable. Studies show that most employees value job satisfaction above money. Sailors are no different. They want to feel appreciated and valued and know they are making a difference. If you want to be a successful leader, challenge your people with goals, tasks, projects and responsibilities that lead to personal success, achievement and accomplishments.

Promise Less and Deliver More

I call this the "Scotty Factor." In the original *Star Trek*, Captain Kirk always needed warp speed in two minutes or the universe would implode. Scotty knew that he could provide warp speed in probably one minute, but he would always say it would be impossible to do it in less than five minutes. Then he would pull through and save the day to great accolades from the captain and crew. He knew all along he could do it in time, but he also knew it would be better if he promised less but delivered more.

Develop a Personal Style of Leadership

Your personal style of leadership is dynamic and can be molded over time. Watch others and you will see both good and bad leaders. Adapt the good traits to your own personal style of leadership and reject the bad. Not only reject them, but also guard your sailors from that negative influence.

In forming my own personal style of leadership over my years of service, I've come to realize a few simple truths. Some might call it wisdom: You can't please everyone. You need thick skin. Mission first, sailors always! You owe your sailors; they don't owe you. If sailors are confused or languishing, you are not doing your job. Do a job right the first time. Your people are your greatest asset. You can delegate authority, but not responsibility. For every problem, be prepared to offer a solution or path to resolution. It's okay to get mad; it's not okay to get mad in view of others. Praise in public, counsel in private. Give credit where credit is due. If two people agree all the time, one of them is not needed. Not only learn from your own mistakes, but learn from the mistakes of others too. You need an honest broker; find someone who isn't afraid to tell you like it is and listen to what they tell you. This job takes relentless preparation. Manage your expectations. Anticipate and expect the unexpected. Find joy in each day: a reason to smile, a reason to laugh.

My bottom line with leadership is that you have to care. You have to want what is best for your country, your people and your organization. If you care enough, live a lifestyle based on the Navy core values of honor, courage and commitment, and make decisions based on those principals. You, your people and your organization will be a success.

Profiles in Patriotic Leadership

BIOGRAPHY

Master Chief Elliott joined the Navy in December 1988 and completed boot camp at San Diego Recruit Training Command as the honor recruit for his class. He graduated Operations Specialist "A" school number one in his class in September 1989 and worked for the remainder of his enlistment in the Public Affairs Office at Dam Neck Naval Base in Virginia Beach, VA. In March 1992 he was released from active duty and moved into the Navy Reserves, assigned to TACRON 24 at Naval Amphibious Base Little Creek. In July 1995 he transferred to Atlantic Fleet Imaging Unit 0186 at Naval Air Reserve Norfolk. Cross-rated to Journalist Second Class in January 1997, he was promoted to First Class Petty Officer later that year. When Imagu 0186 closed its doors in March 2000 he became the Leading Petty Officer at Navy Information Bureau Det 102 at Naval Station Norfolk. In 2002 he was promoted to Chief

48

Greg Slavonic

Petty Officer and ordered to Naval Media Center Fleet Support Detachment as the Senior Enlisted Advisor. When the media center detachment was disestablished In October 2004 he became the Leading Chief Petty Officer at the Navy Office of Information Detachment Fleet Forces Command. In October 2006 he moved to Combat Camera Atlantic as the Leading Chief Petty Officer. He was selected as a Senior Chief Petty Officer in May 2007 and was subsequently assigned as the Senior Enlisted Advisor to the Joint Public Affairs Support Element Reserve unit.

Mobilized to Afghanistan in July 2009 he served as a Task Force Public Affairs Officer and was promoted to Master Chief. His team supported six battalions, a general officer's command staff and multiple coalition partner detachments. Upon his return he was named as the incoming Senior Enlisted Advisor to the Vice Chief of Information in charge of over 200 Sailors.

Master Chief Elliott has traveled the world for the Navy Reserve and many of his photographs have appeared in countless trade publications and military magazines. Among his many assignments were: aboard a submarine to the North Pole, a volunteer for Hurricane Katrina relief efforts and sailing the Baltic Sea. He was the 2003 Naval Reserve Photographer of the Year.

Master Chief Elliott was on the photography staff of The Virginian Pilot newspaper in Norfolk, VA for seven years and is now a freelance commercial and editorial photographer working with USA Today, The New York Times and Navy Times among other national and international publications. He has a Bachelor's Degree in Journalism from Arizona State University.

CHAPTER 4
NOTHING IS EVER AS GOOD OR BAD AS FIRST REPORTED

"In a place where there is leader, do not seek to become a leader. In a place where there is no leader, strive to become a leader."

- The Talmud

Thomas F. Hall, former Assistant Secretary of Defense (Manpower & Reserve Affairs) – Rear Admiral, U.S. Navy (Retired)

Leadership is a strange thing in that it is both relatively simple and complex at the same time. So much has been written about it that it is probably impossible to come up with something new, startling, or revolutionary on the subject. I think one can choose to approach the topic of leadership from an academic or a personal way. Although discussing leadership from the academic angle has many benefits and allows the writer to explore the vast amount of material on questions of: What makes a great leader? What are the attributes of a great leader? What are the basic tenants of leadership? For me, leadership has always been personal, thus, I will stick to providing some of my views of leadership through a few examples of my personal experiences with practical leadership as viewed from the deck plate and hanger deck where I spent a large majority of my 50 years of service to this great nation.

Nothing is ever as good or bad as first reported. I cannot begin to tell you how many times uniformed officers, senior civilians, foreign military and civilian personnel and contractors have either rushed (most of the time, run!) or reluctantly appeared in my office to proclaim that the sky is falling. These are the people I label as having the "Henny Penny complex." Fully well knowing that they only had to be right one time, almost all of the time they were wrong.

On the other end of the spectrum are those that materialize announcing that everything is wonderful; we have just discovered a gold mine; and our products and performance are the greatest ever. I label these people as having the "Pollyanna complex." Most of the time they are wrong. In fact, the vast majority of the time, in almost all organizations both military and civilian, the situation being faced falls somewhere in between the poles of disaster and great success. The leadership point here is that, in my view, the great leaders are the ones able to recognize the magnitude of the situation at hand, preserve calm and see the way ahead. Nothing inspires confidence in an organization as does the calm and effective leader, not panicking, while outlining the course of action. Remember this, aspiring leaders, because I guarantee that you will face it sooner than you might imagine. Resist at all costs being either Henny Penny or Pollyanna, unless the first piece of the sky has already hit you!

Attention to detail is not always fun!

My second example of leadership is one centering on my military experience and is one of advice as much as it is example. Actually, it may have just as much relevance to the civilian world as it does the military. In my experience, the major failure of officers and aspiring civilians that I have observed has been the inability or lack of interest in attention to detail in the administrative and what we all call the paperwork arena. Why? Primarily because it is not fun. It takes time and work and all too many people believe that excellence in this area is not a primary path to success! They mistakenly believe that excellence in this area is not noticed by those running the organization and that it can be left to others, while they have great thoughts to expound upon!

Nothing could be further from the truth. The truth is that many times individuals and organizations are known by their excellence in this arena, and reputations of individuals and organizations are made or lost on how they process paperwork and complete tasks on time and on target. A major failure I have repeatedly encountered in all too many individuals is the lack of advance planning and the realization that just ahead are crises that will undermine one's ability to accomplish the tasks at hand. An advance calendar of at least six months, if not a year, is a hallmark of the good employee, manager and leader. Follow-up, follow-up and more follow-up is absolutely necessary in a dynamic and changing military or civilian environment. Just remember what President Reagan said, "Trust, but verify!" In a most simple way, I told almost all of the people that ever worked for me that when people give you thumbs up that everything is on track, it merely means they have a thumb!

I learned early on while a junior officer and as an aide/military assistant to a very demanding admiral, that I had only one chance to get it right and not embarrass the admiral. It is the basic responsibility of good leaders to understand these principles; practice them; demand advance planning; meet and beat deadlines; lead by example; and have every document superbly written, prepared and representative of the organization. I guarantee you, if you do this; you are on the path to success in establishing not only your personal reputation, but also that of the organization.

Pilots are born, not made!

The third example of leadership that comes to mind is also based on my military experience and is centered on aviation, pilots, and flying in general. Perhaps the general public has a view that all pilots must be well trained and must be "good" in every sense of the word. One could make a case that this is generally true since aviation does have a bit of glamour (just look at **Top Gun** and **The Right Stuff**). Aviators are certainly slow to discourage any view that they and aviation are not glamorous! The fact of the matter is that military aviators do receive superb training throughout their careers. It is therefore tempting to make the leap to the conclusion that all aviators are superb. Such an assumption is not true in my experience, since I really do believe that the truly gifted pilots are born, not made. I might add it is my view that sports are the same. You simply cannot make someone into a Mickey Mantle, Willy Mays, or Larry Bird! Let me explain what is the heart of my argument of leadership in this area.

One of the finest ways to excel as an aviator is to study, learn, know flying and operating procedures, as well as the aircraft, like the back of one's hand. When you combine this with natural ability, the superb aviator results. Again, studying systems and the machine is not always fun (the fun is flying), but it is critical to do both. In my view, the person that knows the machine or product of the company (IT is an example) like the back of one's hand, combined with the innate ability to fly or sell the product, will be successful. It is, thus, the primary responsibility of the good leader to understand this, teach and demand this, and sort out those who can accomplish tasks on a continuing basis that will ensure mission effectiveness or return on investment. Again, through very hard work and training, you can make people into satisfactory pilots, but you cannot make them into superb pilots unless they possess innate ability and want to work.

The same can be said of people in the workplace aspiring to be superb in their profession. I have found that all too many people are willing to accept "just getting by" and only accomplishing what is required to maintain a job and support them or their families. Perhaps in the past, this was acceptable and a way of life. It simply will not work in this most competitive environment in which we now live and probably will pertain for the future.

Living and dying by the choices we make

The fourth example is actually one of advice rather than an example of leadership. It is the one I most frequently use when I speak to groups of school kids and is entitled "Living and Dying by the Choices We Make." At first blush, it is obvious to most of us more mature people that we, in fact, do live and die by the choices we make; but I find it is not as obvious to young people. I well remember when I was a young pilot and preparing to deploy for the first time to the combat zone, we were "bulletproof" and we were going to live forever. Nothing scared us, since we were basically too naïve to be afraid or realize otherwise!

In 1964, I had completed almost a year of flight training, had qualified on an aircraft carrier, had mastered formation flying, and was on top of the world and could not be stopped! It was this way with my fellow students and we were ready for anything. I had just transferred to Corpus Christi, Texas, and my wife Barbara had joined me after completing her teaching obligation in Pensacola, Florida. On one very hot June day, I mounted up in the mighty S-2F two engine training aircraft along with the instructor and my flying partner at that time for our first simulated single engine training flight. The instructor, at some surprise point in the practice landings, would pull the power all the way back on one engine and see how we would do flying the aircraft on just one engine. Of course, the instructor could take the aircraft away from us, add power and use both engines at any point. The first student was to fly the first half of the flight and then switch places with the other student who flew the second half of the flight.

My portion went very well and I switched places with my flying partner. As we flew around the pattern, it was extremely hot, so against regulations and common sense, I made a choice by shedding my flight gloves, helmet and unstrapping and sitting in the aisle of the aircraft in order to see what was happening up front. I might tell you that one thing all S-2F pilots will remember is not to get into a skidded turn stall since more than likely you will spin, crash and probably die! On the first pass at the runway, the student proceeded to approach a skidded turn stall and the instructor barely recovered the aircraft.

At that point, I made the decision that ultimately would determine whether I lived or died on that day. I jumped back in my seat, strapped in as tightly as possible, put on my gloves and helmet and "hunkered down"! On the next pass, the student got us into a skidded turn stall and the instructor did not recover the aircraft. We flipped upside down, did two spins and crashed upside down into Corpus Christi Airport. The aircraft came apart, soaking us with aviation fuel and glass. We slid down the airfield, luckily between the runways on the dirt, which probably saved us from burning. Somehow, I jettisoned the hatch above my seat, exited what was left of the airplane and ran about one half mile from the crash, throwing flight gear as I was chased by some workers in a pickup truck who had observed the crash! I had two bruised knees. The others were not so lucky.

I guess the lesson is obvious. We all live and die by the choices we make. On that day, I made the right choice. Each day after you get up, look in the mirror and ask, "Will I live or die today, and will others, based on the choices I make?" This might change your entire outlook on life.

The line on the wall

I certainly don't want to sound self-serving or boastful when I write about aviation and pilots, but it has been my life. When I was five years old, I pointed up to the sky at a passing airplane and told my mother, "That's what I want to do when I grow up, be a pilot." The path to becoming a pilot was a long way from my family's humble beginnings in Barnsdall, Oklahoma. I believed I was on the road to making my dreams come true when, in the summer of 1959, I hitchhiked into Annapolis, Maryland, in an 18-wheeler (dead broke, out of altitude and airspeed and on my last hope!). I walked the last few miles up West Street to the entrance to the Naval Academy, announced "I am here," and the rest, as they say is history.

Again, as I have repeatedly told the young people to whom I have spoken, "This is the greatest nation on the face of the earth." All you have to do is to have the willingness, the guts and the ambition to succeed; the willingness to work; and those qualities, even combined with average talents, will allow you to find the path to success. I have found there is always someone willing to help those who have the burning desire to work and succeed. I have outlined in this small piece of work some of the pitfalls, principles, ideas and thoughts about leadership and success. I will close, however, with the beginning of my first command tour, that of command of an aviation squadron. For those in military aviation, you know this is the dream of almost every aviator that I have known. It is the thing we aspire to, work towards and make any and every sacrifice to achieve. I might add that, in almost all cases as in mine, it is also the spouse and children that also make many of the sacrifices.

My dream came true when I was honored to assume command of an aviation squadron in 1978. All leaders, military or civilian, whether taking command or control of a military unit or civilian company, generally inherit either a faltering, steady as it goes, or an upward rising organization. I had given the day of assuming command a great deal of thought and throughout my career had been a part of all three types of organizations. I had seen great morale and performance and I had seen great decline and terrible morale. I had seen great commanding officers and ones on the other side. I was blessed with two great commanding officers.

The first was my first Commanding Officer, Rear Admiral (then Commander) Harry Rich. The day I checked into my first squadron, Patrol Squadron Eight, in my welcome aboard interview, he learned that my dear wife was in the hospital 60 miles away facing a spinal operation that could have paralyzed her. Soon after that, he and his wife drove the 120-mile round trip to visit with her in the hospital. That selfless act and caring attitude were something we never forgot, and it demonstrated more than words could say. I decided at that point, if this is what commanding officers are like, I want to be one. Rear Admiral Harry Rich never disappointed me--he was a leader of the highest quality.

My second example was also an admiral, Rear Admiral Ron Marryott. I had not known or served with Admiral Marryott until I made captain and was asked to be his Chief of Staff in Iceland. That assignment seemed a bit daunting to my wife and me, especially when the petty officer arranging our move from Washington, DC, to Keflavik, Iceland, pronounced that, "It isn't the end of the world, but I understand you can see it from there!" Well, nothing could be further from the truth, and the difference was Admiral Ron Marryott. He was a gifted leader; a man of the highest integrity who never forgot a name, and a man who trusted his staff and allowed them to do their jobs. Additionally, he was funny, never took himself too seriously and was an individual that everyone loved to be around. As you might remember, Will Rogers once said, "I never met a man I didn't like." Well, I never met a man who did not like Ron Marryott. The hardest thing I ever had to do was to give this great man's eulogy at his funeral at the United States Naval Academy. The world is not the same without Rear Admiral Ron Marryott.

Soon after my assuming command, as I walked into a meeting with my squadron of 60-plus officers, in a squadron where perhaps some thought "Rome was burning," I thought about what I would say. I said a lot, much of which I wrote down and remember to this day. But perhaps the thing I did that might be the most lasting was simply to go up to the blackboard (we had blackboards with chalk in those days) and draw a simple vertical line. I said to those assembled officers, "This line is what we will all be about." I am sure they must have wondered, "What in the world is this skipper all about – a vertical line?" Then I said: "We will be controlled VP-8 Tigers and no one will beat or defeat us. From this day forward, no one will talk about failure, defeat or giving up; we will compete on the playing fields and win; we will compete in the air and excel; we will charge as hard as humanly possible and will care for each other and for our shipmates.

In doing this, we will have the most fun possible while pushing the safest envelope of flying. From this day forward, no one who wants to be in this squadron will say anything bad about it without a solution to fix it. All of this is contained on the left side of this vertical line. However, on the right side of the line are those who cannot control their drinking and their conduct; those who push the limit of flying into the unsafe area; those who do not care for their shipmates or this squadron; those who have no sense of being their brother's keeper and cannot save others from destroying themselves. They are the kind of people who lie, cheat, and steal. The people on the right side of the line are uncontrolled tigers and have no place here."

I concluded by inviting anyone who could not live by these principles to depart right then and there and to understand that I would have no mercy or forgiveness for those who crossed the line. No one left. We learned and excelled together; we flew safely to the limit; we did not lose an aircraft; we had fun; and we remain comrades and friends today! Enough said!

Greg Slavonic

BIOGRAPHY

Secretary Thomas F. Hall was born December 17, 1939, in Barnsdall, Oklahoma) and sworn in as the fourth Assistant Secretary of Defense for Reserve Affairs on October 9, 2002. A Presidential appointee confirmed by the United States Senate, he serves as the principal staff assistant to the United States Secretary of Defense on all matters involving the 1.2 million members of the Reserve Components of the United States Armed Forces. He is responsible for overall supervision of Reserve Component affairs of the Department of Defense.

Secretary Hall attended Oklahoma State University for one year before entering the United States Naval Academy in Annapolis, Maryland. In 1963, he graduated from the Academy with a bachelor's degree in Engineering and was named as one of the top 25 leaders in his class, having commanded both the top Battalion and Company. He was, also, awarded the Brigade Intramural

Profiles in Patriotic Leadership

Sports Trophy. In 1971, he received a master's degree in Public Personnel Management from George Washington University. He graduated with highest distinction from the Naval War College; with distinction, from the National War College; and from the National Security Course at Harvard University. He was selected as a Fellow and served on the Chief of Naval Operations Strategic Studies Group.

Secretary Hall is a retired two-star Rear Admiral having served almost 34 years of continuous active duty in the United States Navy. He is a distinguished and decorated Naval Aviator, who served a combat tour in Vietnam. He has performed in numerous high level staff, command, and NATO positions during his career. He commanded Patrol Squadron EIGHT, Naval Air Station Bermuda, and dual-hatted as Commander of Fleet Air Keflavik and the Iceland Defense Force. His final military assignment was as the Commander/Director/Chief of Navy Reserve.

His military awards include the Navy Distinguished Service Medal, Defense Superior Service Medal, Legion of Merit, Meritorious Service Medal, Air Medal, and various other personal and unit decorations. He was awarded the Order of the Falcon, with Commander's Cross, by the President of Iceland in recognition of his accomplishments and service as Commander Iceland Defense Force. In 2000, he was given the International Partnership Award for his service to the United States and Iceland. He has been inducted into the Oklahoma Military Hall of Fame. In 2003, he was given the National Service Award for Leadership by the Federal Law Enforcement Foundation. In 2004, he was given the National Citizenship Award by the Military Chaplains Association of the United States of America. In 2005, he was given the Admiral Jackson Award by the Reserve Officers Association.

Greg Slavonic

Secretary Hall has served on the Boards of Directors of numerous nonprofit organizations that support the needs of US veterans and citizens in general. Prior to returning to government service, Secretary Hall served as the Executive Director of the Naval Reserve Association for six years. The Naval Reserve Association is a 501 (c) (3) nonprofit veterans' organization that represents over 23,000 Navy Reserve officers, members, and their families.

CHAPTER 5
LEADERSHIP AIN'T ROCKET SIENCE

"Power tends to corrupt, and absolute power corrupts absolutely."

- Lord Acton

CSM Steve Valley, U.S. Army Reserve

Some people are born leaders, some transform into leaders and some are born to follow leaders. Anyone can give their own description of a strong leader, but it's easier for me to say that I know a strong leader when I see one, just like I can spot a weak leader a mile away.

What I'm going to write was not based on Harvard case studies, but rather by trial and error of an Army senior enlisted leader. It would have been much simpler to sit down and quote from the endless books and manuals on military leadership, but I thought it would be more rewarding to provide real world leadership examples to support my thoughts.

Most of the time war brings out the best in leaders and future leaders, but that doesn't mean that the war time military leader is infallible. The military is made up of volunteers and therefore, is reflective of society and vulnerable to the same kinds of shortcomings in values and beliefs that plague the rest of the country. However, in my opinion these shortcomings are at a miniscule rate compared to the rest of the civilian population. The U.S. military is held to a higher standard not only because of our stellar history of defending democracy and fighting for what is right, we're held to a higher standard because we demand it.

You'd need two lifetimes to read all the books written on leadership, but strong effective leadership can be thrown out the window without the basic core values of honesty and accountability. A leader can be a great motivator and the most proficient soldier in the platoon, but if they don't practice and live with honesty and accountability in not only their professional lives, but in their personal lives, then the end result will ultimately be failure.

For example, Bernie Madoff appeared to be a financial genius that earned his clients unmatched financial fortunes for decades, but in the end his long stream of dishonesty put him on the fast track to a financial failure and a lengthy prison term. Only after he was caught did he become somewhat accountable for his actions, although the clients who collectively lost billions of dollars may have a different opinion on this subject.

Semper Gumby

One aspect of duty that war time leaders have to deal with more than any other leader whether in government or the private sector is change. I've said many times that there is no organization that handles change more professionally and effectively than the U.S. military; and it's primarily because the competent leaders that are responsible implement these sometimes daily changes in regulations and strategies. These same leaders may not initially agree with the changes they implement, but they know that their own survival, and more importantly the survival of the men and women they lead depend on their ability to transform their leadership to ensure success.

One of the more recent issues that military leaders dealt with was the repeal of the Don't Ask, Don't Tell (DADT) policy. The country was ready for the huge blowback from the military when DADT policy was rescinded last year because of the buildup of controversy during its Congressional vote. Well, the policy came and went and military operations didn't miss a beat. The mainstream media were preparing for anti-gay protests and controversial statements from military members but in reality every military member from the top down received excellent training on the policy change so when it did happen it was barely noticed by the military and civilians alike.

Part of succeeding as a military leader in war is being able to immediately alter course or strategy, whether on the front lines or in garrison. Yes, corporate and governmental leaders are also able to adapt to change, but usually after an extended period of time where official plans or strategy is created, analyzed and finally implemented weeks or sometimes months after the initial proposal. However, I've not seen an organization with the ability to change strategy during the middle of an active operation like the military.

The past 10 years of war have created a large pool of battle hardened leaders that faced multiple year-long deployments in combat zones. Though we tell ourselves that we train and lead the same way in garrison than we do in a combat zone, the stark reality is that we don't. Leaders have a tendency to not worry about the "ankle biters" because it's life and death in the streets of Baghdad or Kabul, and you don't need to stay on top of many of the regulations that most of us grew up with during our military careers.

I'm not saying that the Army has become a force of reckless hooligans, but we'd be kidding ourselves if we didn't admit that we've become lax in enforcing some regulations that were the norm in garrison. The choice was easy for me when confronted with making sure one of your soldier's uniform is up to standards or worrying about ammo for a scheduled convoy in downtown Baghdad.

However, NCOs (Non Commissioned Officers) must now change course and get back to the basics of discipline and training now that we're beginning to transition out of Afghanistan and heading out of war into a more traditional home station training schedule.

I've had the opportunity to lead in combat arms units, as well as rear support elements in the public affairs world, and I can tell you that leadership styles in a field unit is 180 degrees different from leading soldiers in a garrison outfit.

Leadership consisted of receiving the mission at hand and instructing a lower enlisted soldier to get it done back in my days of being a being a rifleman in an infantry platoon and serving in a field artillery battery. I can remember being on the receiving end of countless orders to dig a foxhole in a field of rocks, conduct a recon over a hill filled with briar patches or pack everything up because we've got to move to a new firing position in 30 mikes.

When you gave or received these orders there were no questions or comments that came with it. It was understood by the platoon sergeant and private first class alike that this is what the mission was, no questions asked. There was complete trust in your leader knowing what was best and what he wanted he got. Once an order was given, the soldier did an about face and went to work. What the man wanted the man got, no questions. The infantry is hard charging and the only direction they move is forward.

Move ahead several years from the field to a public affairs detachment that primarily worked in garrison and I noticed the change in leadership style my first day when I watched an Army private question an order that his sergeant gave to him. I looked on as the private fired several questions back to the sergeant about the mission. I watched the conversation in virtual shock.

Public affairs is a niche military occupational specialty (MOS) that requires a minimum 110 GT score (verbal score combined with arithmetic) on the Armed Services Vocational Aptitude Battery (ASVAB) along with the ability to obtain at least a Department of Defense secret security clearance, so right off the bat you know that your subordinates are going to be a little smarter and inquisitive than a traditional combat arms soldier.

Although I was considered a junior NCO myself as a staff sergeant, I was ready to pounce on that private for questioning the legitimacy of an order that his first line leader gave to him. Luckily, I didn't enter the conversation but instead watched the scenario progress until the sergeant sent the young man off to perform the mission.

I approached the sergeant and asked him why he allowed a private to question his authority and the legitimacy of what appeared to be a simple mission. The sergeant told me that the way I led in a combat arms unit wouldn't work in public affairs because the soldiers were of a different breed. Whereas a grunt was brought up to do whatever needed to be done without questioning the origins of the mission, a public affairs soldier was trained in an atmosphere that encouraged questioning all facets of a mission before accepting the responsibility of performing the duty.

It wasn't a matter of disrespect, it was the different culture or mindset of these two military occupational specialties and if I didn't allow my leadership style to evolve or transform to the public affairs or a rear support environment then I would end up failing as a public affairs leader and almost assuredly end up back in the field as an Infantryman.

This didn't mean that I couldn't hold my subordinates accountable for their actions, but it did mean that the days of barking out orders and expecting them all to be acted on without questions or comments were over. What I originally viewed as a lack of respect or discipline by a private, was just another challenge in leadership style because of the different make up of soldiers from a line unit to those in a purely support role.

I continue to serve as a public affairs soldier today so I think you can pretty much tell from this statement that the required leadership style transformation was made that allow me to serve some 19 years later.

Lead from the Front

There was a quote I pulled out of the Washington Post and hung on my office wall shortly after I arrived in Baghdad in January, 2004. Then Maj. Gen. David Petraeus was commander of the 101st Airborne Division and was redeploying back to Ft. Campbell, KY, after a successful mission leading the Screaming Eagles in the 2003 Iraqi invasion. The quote read, "Always lead from the front, except in the chow hall."

To a civilian or junior soldier the words didn't mean much, but to an Army First Sergeant leading a group of more than 70 Soldiers, Airmen, Marines and civilians in Baghdad it was the tenet of my wartime leadership philosophy.

My translation of this simple quote made me think of a couple important characteristics of military leadership that were instilled in me throughout my military career.

First, there is the basic rule that a leader never asks his subordinates to do something that he cannot do him or herself. Lead from the front.

I can't tell you how many times I witnessed an officer or a senior NCO task a soldier with a mission that they had never been assigned or completed themselves. I remember the first time I had to order a young soldier run a convoy on Route Irish, more commonly known as Airport Road (the most dangerous 10-mile stretch of roadway in the world circa 2004-2005). What made this decision easier for me was the fact that I made sure that I was the first unit member to be in a convoy assignment for our unit from the Green Zone to Camp Victory.

This wasn't a deep, thought out process. It was a leader's natural first reaction and the decision was made in the blink of an eye. It was what Army leaders have done for 237 years; it was leading by example and showing my assigned personnel that I wouldn't assign them something that I've never done. This also showed that the convoy mission was important enough to rate the First Sergeant volunteering for it so the rest of the unit would see the importance of future convoy missions that never stopped during our 12-months in Baghdad.

The other leadership trait that glared at me from the quote that my soldiers were not only first in line at the chow hall, but for virtually everything else we had to endure lines for in Baghdad.

One of the military's favorite sayings is that we "Rush to Wait." We move at 100 miles per hour in everything we do, but it never fails that we still end up waiting in lines no matter how efficient we really are. A military leader always ensures that his/her soldiers are first in line, while the leader always brings up the rear. A leader always takes care of his troops first before satisfying his own personal needs

I remember arriving at the Republican Palace in Baghdad and immediately dropping my gear off at my bunk and then heading to my new office while everyone else stayed behind. Truth be told, I would have much rather took the afternoon off to square away my bunk and get some rest, but my commander had previously told me that we'd have no time off until the both of us set the whole unit up for success.

The two of us worked with the unit we relieved to make personnel and other key decisions while the rest of the unit was able to eat and call home (which I ordered them to do through a free phone call from a dedicated State Department telephone line). Being a leader means not doing the easy thing when nobody expects you do anything but.

Yes, our initial efforts provided the core of long term success, but one immediate reward of our leadership philosophy of unit first was that our bunks were already made by the time we returned from our duty and this made our initial life easier as we embarked on our life in Baghdad. It may not have been much, but it was needed and appreciated.

Never Stop Learning

There's a reason why the US military has been called the most educated and professional fighting force in the world. It's because we are.

The first time I knew that a professional education was integral to success in the Army was during my first years in the Massachusetts Army National Guard. I had the pleasure of serving under the tutelage of Captain Paul Giguere in Alpha Company, 2/104th Infantry. The "Old Man" was a construction foreman in the civilian world and a complete soldier once he donned the Army BDU.

Captain Giguere earned respect from us the right way by being a proficient, well informed Infantry Soldier, but the one facet he was missing in his career was a college degree. He was eventually told by the battalion commander that he wouldn't be promoted any higher because he was not a college graduate. Never mind that he was born to be a leader of men, if he didn't have a college degree his career was red flagged.

Jump forward twenty years and you'd have a hard time finding anyone in the officer ranks, but also in the NCO Corps that hasn't enrolled or graduated from an associate's or bachelor's degree program in any part of the world where our warriors serve and the results are simply astounding.

I received tuition reimbursement and the student loan repayment option when I signed my first enlistment contract in 1985. I parlayed this original contract into additional educational benefits from the Defense Activity for Non-Traditional Educational Support (DANTES) that provided me tuition assistance that assisted me in paying for my Master's Degree from Boston College.

I had an advanced civilian degree and the first phase of the Army's First Sergeant Course completed by the time I deployed to Baghdad in 2004. If you combine my education with my civilian and military background in the public affairs spectrum, I doubt you could find another soldier that had as much public affairs experience as me in the whole country of Iraq. I'm not saying that I was the best military public affairs practitioner, but I am saying that my resume of experience as an Army senior enlisted leader would have matched up bullet point by bullet point with any public affairs soldier, officer or enlisted, in Iraq

Upon taking a look at the decentralized decision making paradigm that was instituted at the origins of Operations Enduring and Iraqi Freedom more than 10 years ago; never before in the history of the US military have so many young soldiers been trusted to make as many key strategic decisions as they have in

Afghanistan and Iraq. I'm not talking about the junior and company grade officers making these snap war-time decisions, I'm talking about the 18-20 year old enlisted soldier that is able to conduct a lightning fast analysis of the conditions and render a decision that can mean the saving or taking of a life, can be the flashpoint for an international incident, coming to an agreement with the elders of a peace "Jirga" in an Afghan village or the funding of a community development program worth hundreds of thousands of dollars.

It's expected that senior soldiers at my level are to make these types of rational decisions based on experience and situational analysis learned through the different levels of leadership we've all endured. However, what we've asked our youngest warriors to do in making these types of senior leader decisions is a direct attribute to the Army's commitment to the Non-Commissioned Officer Education System (NCOES) and of course the push to match the military training with a civilian education.

This learning never stops because unlike the civilian or governmental sectors, a NCO will not be considered for promotion until they complete the next level of NCOES. When I was promoted to Sergeant Major in 2006; the promotion was contingent on my graduating from the U.S. Army Sergeants Major Academy, which I did in 2009.

There's not another profession in the world (corporate or governmental) that allows such junior or inexperienced employees to take the lead and make a decision, and more than 99-percent of the time, the right decision, that could have a direct effect on the survival of a corporation of governmental agency or cause an international crisis like the Army does.

In my opinion there's no better example of a successful decentralized leadership model than what the US Army has instituted during the past decade of war. And that's why America will be in good hands for the foreseeable future because we've got a brand new generation of great leaders just waiting for the opportunity to showcase their military learned talents to the rest of the world.

Walk Around Leadership

I was lectured by a very talented Marine colonel many years ago that one of the most important aspects of being an effective leader is to spend a few hours each week conducting walk around leadership in your unit so that your troops could see the human part of you, not just the senior leader barking out orders from the front of a formation or the issuer of punishment from behind a desk in my office.

Fortunately I took this guidance to heart and brought it to a higher level by practicing in on a daily basis for most of my tour in Baghdad. It wasn't that I had to know everything that was going on with every section in my unit; it was mainly to show the people I led that I was interested in their daily survival.

My goal in this practice was not to become best friends with my soldiers, but to provide them the one on one contact with their senior leader that was sometimes neglected because the high operational tempo in Baghdad.

I made it a point to ask about their families back home and what missions they were working on, but never told them how I would go about getting the job done unless I was asked by them for guidance. I realized that just because I did a mission a certain way didn't mean that my way was the only way. Younger soldiers were taught new processes during training and it was up to me to understand that their way was better for them, even though I still thought that my way was more effective. I surmised that as long as the job was done right and deadlines were met then all was good.

However, I made it clear early on to my soldiers that everyone learned from mistakes. I had no problem with one of my soldiers making a mistake, with the understanding that the same mistake would not be made a second time. I would take the shrapnel from our chain of command the first time a mission didn't go as planned as any senior leader is taught to do. But the second time a mistake was made on the same mission is where the hammer would come down and where I would implement my own way to complete the mission.

More recently, Command Sergeant Major Frank Grippe, the senior enlisted leader at U.S. Central Command (CENTCOM) conducted the same walk around leadership strategy during a 10-day war exercise conducted at CENTCOM headquarters. Grippe made sure that he visited the Joint Operations Center on a daily basis to talk to every person and shake their hand whether military or civilian during the exercise. I took the time to commend him on this action and he replied that it was nothing special; it's what we're expected to do as senior leaders.

NCOs are the backbone of the Army

I can't tell you how many times I've heard this quote during my 26-year Army career. I'm sure the first person to tell me this important fact was one of my two senior drill sergeants at basic combat training at Ft. Benning, GA in 1985.

While I don't think any soldier, whether enlisted or officer, can dispute the statement, I think today's NCOs have evolved from being the backbone of the Army into becoming a valued shared strategic partner that the Army cannot survive without in today's multi-faceted strategic environment.

NCOs have historically been the doers in the Army. The officers were, and still are seen as the leaders who make the big plans that the NCOs are tasked with carrying out. I don't think this is a negative connotation on NCOs, but we've grown considerably over the past two decades to the point that we're involved in that actual planning of strategy, not just the tactical details of getting the job done. In today's environment, problems or even failure can be almost guaranteed when an officer doesn't engage his senior enlisted leader in every stage of the planning process of an operation.

Parting Shots

My commander in Baghdad invited one of her friends from the Special Forces community to stay with us in Baghdad during an official visit after our unit had been in theater for about six months. This Army colonel led a psychological operations battalion and had a great talent in conducting informal personality analyses for people he found interesting.

I had no idea that he was doing this in my case until he pulled me aside one day and said that my leadership style was effective because I liked to keep people off balance. Upon further discussion he explained that he watched me deal with my soldiers on various issues for a couple days and was impressed with the way I handled the multitude of issues and missions.

The colonel said that one of the reasons why my soldiers performed well is that I kept them off balance with my reactions to a particular subject. When I told my wife this finding she laughed and called it plain old moodiness!

The colonel told me that most soldiers already know what's going to enrage their senior leaders, but that wasn't the case with me. What would set me off one day wouldn't even register a blip the next day and this was beneficial to the point that my soldiers were not hesitant to approach me with problems because of any preordained views that I may have had. I had no idea I was doing it but appreciated the colonel's assessment that it worked and I still do it subconsciously to this day.

I've discussed several ingredients to effective leadership in this essay but what it all boils down to may be as simple as what an Army major passed on during my first days in Baghdad.

He said, "First Sergeant, there's three things you can't mess up as a leader, if you get them right then you'll be fine. Don't screw with a soldier's mail, pay or chow and you'll be fine." *And truer words were never spoken.*

BIOGRAPHY

Steve Valley is a 26-year Army Reserve and National Guard veteran. He's qualified in several military occupational specialties including 11B infantry, 13E field artillery and 46Z public affairs. Steve currently serves in the U.S. Army Reserve as a Command Sergeant Major with the 205th Public Affairs Operation Center. He previously served as the Public Affairs Chief at US Forces-Japan and as the deputy Sergeant Major of Army Public Affairs at the Army Office of the Chief of Public Affairs at the Pentagon.

Steve is currently employed as a defense contractor performing duties as a Media Analyst for the Central Command Communication Integration Division at U.S. Central Command Headquarters in Tampa, FL. His civilian sector career also includes tenures in public affairs/relations management with the Tampa Port Authority, Raymond James Financial Corporate Headquarters, Bisk Education and the Massachusetts Housing Finance Agency.

Steve's former Army Reserve unit returned from a year-long deployment to Iraq in February 2005, where he served as the unit's first sergeant, the senior enlisted soldier at the Combined Press Information Center (CPIC) and as a media spokesperson for Multi-National Forces-Iraq.

Steve's book, *Inside the Fortress*, was published in November 2009 by American Book Publishing and is for sale at Amazon.com as a paperback and ebook.

He's been honored as an All-American VFW Post Commander and serves on the Executive Board of the Suncoast Chapter of the Association of the US Army (AUSA), the American Legion, the Employers Support for the Guard and Reserve (ESGR) and is a sustaining member of the USO, the Warrior Legacy Foundation and the Wounded Warrior Project.

CHAPTER 6

ABOUT GETTING THINGS DONE

*"Remember praise is more valuable
than blame."*

- General George S. Patton, Jr.

Major John Wagner, U.S. Army Reserve

When I was approached to write for this project, I was asked to consider all aspects of leadership experience in my theme. There were no constraints on it, and that I didn't necessarily have to follow the previous book in developing it. With that kind of open forum, what I had to consider was pretty damn broad. So I wanted to look at doing something that remained broad, and hopefully inject it into what we should consider 'leadership'. Especially given that we are entering a phase in our history where who we choose to be our next government leader could have a substantial effect for a very long time to come.

I grew up exposed to all different kinds of leadership styles- from autocratic follow-the-book types, to the ones that wanted only 'to do what's right'. Even a few that basically knew the 'rules' were only there to be broken or re-written. And that latter type seemed to be the most effective leadership style. Which type are we going to end up with come November, 2012? I submit that we are going to have to choose between two distinctly different styles- an education-based, no direct-leadership-experience type, and a primarily business type of leader.

Here it is, approaching the summer of 2012, and we have to examine exactly which of these types of leadership styles we are going to need for the next 4, possibly 8, years. In my mind, we need the one that's going to see what we need to do, and given the framework of the Constitution, go get it done. They will have to re-examine what we currently have, and then fix what is apparently very, very broken. A good leader will be able to identify the greatest needs quickly, assess priorities, and set about to getting things done.

In our history, we seem to adapt to selecting which type of leader is needed at the time more than we realize. For the most part, the collective bloc of voters seemed to be influenced by economic and defensive conditions as much as any entirely political considerations. Simply put, selecting Washington as the first leader was the only real choice at the time as he was a tested military leader who could get things done. Following up with Adams and Jefferson, who had no military background akin to Washington, their election was considerable as much for their intelligence and experience in law as other factors. Jefferson, particularly, was one that could set the standard going forward on how best to govern what he had written; Washington was the 'implementer'. In the military, you find that leadership styles of leaders put to individual units tend to sway back and forth. You may get some 'bookish' leaders at one stage, and more 'tactical' leaders at others. What has this to do with now? We are, in my opinion, in the need of a 'tactical' leadership style.

I'm not talking about someone who is going to man-up and try to wipe out the Taliban or get us into some other campaign in the Middle East. I'm talking about someone who's going to do this domestically—who is going to see that we have a 'broken' situation in nearly every way (business productivity, regulation, deficits, healthcare, etc.) and be willing to lead into doing something about it. For the first time in a long time, we may end up having to choose between leaders who have never been tested by the military. Thinking back among all the elections since Roosevelt, name one where neither candidate has served in the military?

Reagan-Dukakis? No- Dukakis served in Korea.

Bush-Clinton? Please. We all know Bush (both of them) served.

How about Nixon-Johnson? False. Nixon served in WWII.

This puts us in a unique position in this election- not since the Roosevelt-Dewey campaigns of 1944 has neither candidate for President had military service. For the first time in several generations, we have to look at the leadership style we are selecting from in a perspective in which neither candidates have been 'tested' in one of our more traditional way—by serving in some capacity in uniform. This will be a very unique perspective in which to measure our potential leader.

But why is this important? Why is this trait or experience something that would matter in politics, especially now?

"To become truly great, one has to stand with people, not above them."

— Charles de Montesquieu

What we have to consider is the totality of being in situations that test, hone, and build the character of the person; the ability to make decisions based not only on some committee, but also on the maturity of the person making the decision. Most that have not had military experience have not matured their thought process far enough to face such complex and tough decisions. The second and third order effects are sometimes as important as the immediate one; combined, those affects can be longer-term than one you're facing now. In business, usually the totality of leader decisions means the loss of money—either revenue, expenses, or market. Those can usually be recovered, with no life jeopardized. In politics, while lives can be affected, in the U.S. it's very rare that leadership would affect immediate loss of life, beyond disasters or the president's military decisions. But as a military leader, your immediate, and tertiary, decisions can affect lives in ways that are irreparable. That tests your wits in ways very few ever consider. That maturity level, even if gained while relatively young, pays dividends that we need and need now.

In my 31 years of wearing a uniform, with experience from the squad level to the national level of leadership, I've seen many who were so outside their ability that it was hard to understand how they reached their position. From the company commander who could not make decisions in complex situations, to the state commander who had such little regard for those that worked for him that once he was due to leave, no one wanted to attend his retirement. With vetting that goes on in most political situations, such a 'leader' would not rise to the level of consideration for national politics.

The downside of military experience is that it has the tendency to burn you out. Over-working and depleting your energy level to such an extent that you want nothing to do with further responsibility. But those that rise above this, prosper, and move on are truly exceptional and worthy of political consideration. That's part of the vetting process that the military experience provides that we need to see today. Who has the ability to face such complex, stressful, and important decisions and has the background to implement them?

What we are facing today is as unique as it is immediate. The drawdown of Vietnam isn't the only situation we need to look at here and compare to—we need to look at the leadership more recently, during the time of the end of the Cold War. We are facing a situation where the Cold War will be looked upon as neater, more orderly, with more gamesmanship akin to a chess board. Today's 'Overseas Contingency Operations' are proving to be more kinetic, more frenzied, and shorter-lived than anything during the Cold War era. This difference will require someone who can make a decision quickly, with conviction, and not break the law. That decision-making capability is typically honed only in the military.

Politically, we choose leaders who tend to be cooperation-based, educated, visionary, but tested.

Without the background of some military training, can we say a political leader minus that piece of background is fully capable? Has been tested properly? I'm not stepping out here and saying that every military leader is fit for politics; far from it. In many cases some of the military 'leaders' I've faced should never have been in uniform, let alone selected for senior positions. But the military at least brings out that missing element that you can point to, with the intended effect of saying, 'no, not this one' when the proper time arrives (say, an election.)

During my years in uniform, and especially as my time as an officer (I am a 'mustang', having entered the military as a Private) my leadership training went from intense in the early years to nearly non-existent by the time I reached Field Grade. Your education and learning capacity was of greater emphasis rather than your ability to direct and coordinate others; staff operations became the norm. This is a turning point that I find as a failure in the current military. While Ranger Schools and other Infantry-type training emphasizes skills, and the NCO-based schools do as well, the de-emphasis of developing strong instincts on leadership vice staff capability can only hurt in the long run. What with the coming drawdown of troops and end-strength in the military though, you can rightly assume that there will be more staff positions than troop-facing one by a greater margin.

While nothing develops leadership more than combat (I don't care which field—successful combat begets good leaders) it seems as if today's military will be facing another end-of-Vietnam scenario: empty experience from most of those that remain while those with the 'real' experience are pushed out because they didn't get a 'checkmark' in the schoolbook since they were serving tours.

That brings us back to the current scenario—where neither of the potential leaders of this country have had any military experience whatsoever. Worse, no one in their family has had any, either, so they even lack the 'atmospherics' of even being exposed to the military setting. This further removes them, and the military, from understanding each other, and being better able to work together on what is needed for the country. While civilian leadership will always be the norm for the military, at least having someone who can identify with, or better relate to, those who have served is something we desire. Having that ability to cut across both the uniformed and non-uniformed populace gains respect and understanding. While respect for a specific rank in the military is automatic, respect for the INDIVIDUAL in that rank in the service is earned- up to and including the President.

I think we need to take a very hard look at who we are vetting and selecting for such an important leadership position and I think, coming up in at least 2020 that will happen. By then, today's combat vets will be ready to assume more civilian leadership roles in politics, and we should have another round of good, strong, TESTED individuals from the ranks that can lead America. And we won't face an un-tested, inexperienced leadership again.

Greg Slavonic

BIOGRAPHY

Mr. Wagner is a native of Athens, Ohio and graduated from Ohio University in 1985. He was commissioned via ROTC as a 2nd Lieutenant the same year and has extensive experience in both the military and as a civilian professional. Mr. Wagner recently served in the Colorado National Guard, assigned to USNORTHCOM and currently holds the rank of Major.

He has 31 years in Active Duty, Reserve, and National Guard service and 22 straight months in Iraq and Kuwait. While deployed to OIF (Operation Iraqi Freedom) I and II, he served in various positions on the staffs of CJTF (Commander Joint Task Force) 7 and MNF-I commanders. His assignments included handling media during Saddam Hussein's arraignment, numerous press conferences, and serving as the Intelligence Liaison to the Interim Iraqi Government. He developed U.S. media strategy for addressing anti-coalition press and propaganda in Arab media during the battles of al Najaf and Fallujah, as well as many other special assignments in Baghdad. He received a Bronze Star Medal for actions in combat in Baghdad.

After his return from Baghdad, Mr. Wagner was heavily involved in Hurricane Katrina relief efforts, where he led and developed the briefings for the Joint Chiefs and the Secretary of Defense for the commander of US NORTHCOM. He also worked in the coordination of relief efforts among all the major US agencies: Army Corps of Engineers, FEMA, Homeland Security, as well as Red Cross and other supporting agencies.

In civilian life, he is a founding partner and former CTO for an airline based overseas, and has also worked as an independent IT consultant. He is an experienced leader and technologist with over twenty years of experience in Information Technology within the Fortune 100, to include well-known companies: Accenture, IBM, WorldCom, Sprint, Ford Motor, Marriott Hotels, DuPont, Caterpillar, and Time Warner Telecom. He has spearheaded business development solutions in Asia for many companies.

In the Defense industry, Mr. Wagner worked with Boeing Systems as a lead consultant for the Future Combat Systems development on the C4ISR and Unmanned Aerial Vehicle platforms, developing and assisting with integration models and methods.

Mr. Wagner is heavily involved in the development of "New Media" - he writes for one of the largest and most awarded military blogs (milblogs) on the Internet: www.BlackFive.net, and has been a contributing writer to Pajamas Media, Breitbart's Big

Greg Slavonic

Peace, and other outlets. A current project is to help a new software company start-up engage in the New Media space and obtain funding for operations.

He has served as the Director/Campaign Manager for a major US Senate campaign, where he developed strategy, campaign staffing initiatives, as well as press and media/new media strategies. While the candidate was not successful, it allowed Mr. Wagner to develop wide ranging contacts in Colorado media circles.

Mr. Wagner was involved in the forming and founding of a new Veterans Service Organization and think tank: The Warrior Legacy Foundation / Warrior Legacy Institute. This group was established to assist both veterans and veterans groups, and already has over 55,000 members across the US. Mr. Wagner serves on the Board of the Foundation and serves as its interim director. He is also a founding partner of a company whose focus is to bring soldier-related content to both new media and "legacy media" outlets. This new company, called SOG Media (Special Observers Guild) is currently in negotiations with studios to develop a 26-episode series, titled "*Faces of Valor*."

Mr. Wagner has an extensive background in public speaking and addressing the media. He has been interviewed on CNN, Fox, BBC, AP, Cavuto, as well as many other publications around the world. He has interviewed with the *NY Times, Washington Post, Dallas Morning News, LA Times,* and other regional publications. He has been a featured speaker for US Congressmen and Senators, as well as many large corporations. He speaks on a variety of issues, from technology to the military, to his experiences overseas.

CHAPTER 7

PRINCIPLES OF RESPONSIBILITY AND LEADERSHIP

"Success is to be measured not so much by the position that one has reached in life as by the obstacles which he has overcome."

- Booker T. Washington

Lieutenant General Don Wetekam, U.S. Air Force (Retired)

It is clear from the events of the last few years that American business needs to revitalize its commitment to strong ethical standards. When faced with somewhat similar circumstances in the 1970s, the U.S. Air Force met this challenge by focusing on responsibility and accountability within the service to produce a fighting force that was able to prevail in Operation Desert Storm and beyond.

Many years ago, at the suggestion of one of my mentors, I began to keep a file of quotations and sayings that I would read or hear in various places that had a certain appeal. If I heard something that really spoke to me, I would write it down and then later transfer it to a master file. As time went on, I added humorous anecdotes, excerpts from various speeches and book passages that I thought might have value in the future or simply caught my attention for whatever reason. What started as a paper file eventually made its way onto a floppy disk and then onto various other electronic storage devices as technology advanced. Today that file is rather lengthy and contains quotes, jokes, stories, and words of wisdom that I have used frequently during formal public speaking engagements as well as casual conversations.

But more important than the fact that I can now punch up my speeches with some decent jokes, catchy sayings, or inspiring words from some noted figure, I have found that this collection has acted as a sort of personal balance throughout the years as I faced a variety of challenges. Periodically, I still reflect on some of these words and how they relate to things we all face every day. Since I amassed most of the file while I was serving in the military, it's naturally weighted heavily toward that profession. Nonetheless, I have found that the insights contained in many of those excerpts have widespread application in the business world as well. It never hurts to reconsider the wisdom that some of the world's great leaders have offered over the years. So recently, as I read through that file yet once again, I came upon an excerpt that caught my attention. I had long forgotten about this particular quotation, and when I read it I had to pause and reconsider in light of recent events. It speaks to what I perceive as a troubling unwillingness of many public leaders to accept responsibility for their actions, especially some in the business community. I say troubling because it is a trend that seems to be growing with each passing year, and that is cause for concern as we think about the future of our nation and our society.

Before I go any further, it might be beneficial to lay out a little background on the source. Military veterans of Desert Storm will undoubtedly be familiar with General Chuck Horner. General Horner was the commander of the coalition Air Forces during Operation Desert Storm in 1991, arguably one of the most successful air campaigns in history. Some may recall seeing him at the briefing podium on the evening news, describing video clips from the previous day's air action and explaining specific operations. A great majority of those who watched him in that setting found him personable and well-versed on his topic, with a strong and commanding presence. Those of us in uniform knew him as a leader who took his responsibility for the success of that operation very seriously.

I served under General Horner back in the late 1980s when I was a squadron commander at one of the bases under his command. He was not known for a spit-and-polish image. In fact, some may have described him as a bit unkempt in his appearance and a bit quirky as well. He was, however, known for thoroughness, common sense, and strong perceptive skills. His area of responsibility included not only all the fighter bases in the Eastern U.S., but also U.S. air operations in the Middle East for any contingency that might arise. He took both roles very seriously and thus he immersed himself in the Middle Eastern region and its military. So as the U.S. Air Force prepared for combat operations against Iraq in late 1990 and early 1991, those of us on the inside took quiet confidence in the man that we knew would lead the operation. As history has come to show, that confidence was well placed.

Novelist Tom Clancy profiled General Horner and other Air Force leaders of that era in his 1999 book, *Every Man a Tiger*. I read that book with particular interest because I grew up as a young officer in the post-Vietnam Air Force, and much of what Clancy described in his work centered on the leadership lessons that we all learned during that era. One passage from that book that made it into my quotations file was directly from General Horner:

"If you want responsibility, if you want the tough jobs, then you better be ready to stand up and take the criticism and all the anguish when things go wrong. If you can't take the blame – even for mistakes that are beyond your control – then you are not in a responsible job, no matter what the job title says. The big jobs involve risk of great personal criticism. The jobs worth having are the ones with the biggest downside, and if you don't admit your own mistakes, you are not worthy of the trust given to you.

"...to seek credit for a job well done while ducking the pain and disgrace of failure is not leadership."

As I came across that particular passage recently, I paused. I was troubled as I tried to relate General Horner's words to actions I have witnessed in more recent years from a number of people in leadership roles, particularly some in the business community who attained notoriety for less-than-ethical practices. And I wondered how we seemingly have moved so far from those words that so accurately describe principles of responsibility and leadership that often seem to be lacking in the world around us.

Our global economy is still recovering from the difficulties that began in 2008 with the collapse of some of the world's largest financial institutions, and that recovery will likely take several more years. Like many I was surprised and disheartened by the apparent lack of accountability that followed many of the stories concerning these failed businesses. Some of those stories involve criminal activity so I need to be clear here. I'm not talking about that; it's not the focus of this article. To me, that's the easy stuff. The news media is full of stories of former officials who knowingly violated statutes and/or participated in covering up the details once problems started to arise. There's no dilemma here – illegal activity should begat swift, substantial punishment under the law. It's cut and dried. What I'm talking about here is the lack of moral leadership and accountability that may still be technically permissible under the law. It's about ethical standards in the business community.

I should also add that the large preponderance of business leaders that I have met and worked with both during my years in the military and more recently in private industry are strongly-principled people of high moral character. I'm fortunate to work among a group who set and demand high standards of business ethics. I wouldn't have it any other way. But as the business world continues to change and as the investment horizons of many continue to shrink, I worry about the trends and I wonder how people of strong moral purpose can continue to thrive in this environment.

With that question in mind, let me try to relate to some of my experiences in the military. I've been witness to a pronounced shift in public opinion over the last 40 years relating to public perceptions of many of our institutions to include both the military and business. When I first entered active duty military service in the early 1970s, the military usually ranked at or near the bottom of public opinion polls of our most trusted institutions. Today the military receives some of the highest ratings with public confidence levels that far exceed those for the federal government, business, and the legal profession to name just a few. How did this happen? What occurred to raise the public's perception of the military, and how have other once-respected institutions like American business fallen so far?

Let me begin by concentrating on the first part of the question: What occurred to improve the public's perception of the military? And I will approach that from my own experience. I entered the U.S. Air Force Academy as a cadet in 1969. The military was not particularly popular or respected at that time. The nation was in the throes of the Vietnam War, and despite the overall unpopularity of the war and the draft, I believe the poor public regard for the military stemmed primarily from a lack of moral leadership and honesty among some within the senior military ranks rather than the war itself. I recall listening to the evening news reports throughout the late 1960s, and all too frequently there were reports of improprieties involving senior military leaders. There were enemy "body count" figures which seemed grossly inflated. Then there was the tragic My Lai massacre and the subsequent attempts by some to cover up that event.

Add to that several other incidents and you have a situation where the senior ranks of the U.S. military were perceived as not being truthful or accepting of responsibility.

That was the Air Force that I entered in 1969. And while the Academy curriculum included a heavy focus on ethical standards as crucial part of officer training, I didn't perceive that focus as being strongly reinforced within the operational Air Force that I entered upon graduation four years later. Many leaders of that era recognized we had a problem not only with the service's public image but with our own internal standards of conduct, and they were starting to push to regain the ethical high ground. But that didn't happen overnight. As I recall, the 1970s were one long, hard struggle in that regard.

Adding to the problem was the fact that we simply were not a very effective air force during those years. But technical capability was only part of the problem. Many like to distill the problems around the "hollow force" of the '70s down to the simple fact that much of the equipment the Air Force and the other services operated was old and worn out by the Vietnam War. But the issue wasn't just about buying new equipment. In fact the average age of the aircraft in the U.S. Air Force today is more than double that of the mid-70s, but today's Air Force is considerably more effective in terms of its ability to deliver capability for America than that earlier version. I believe the root of the turnaround that began in the late 1970s was marked by a singular focus on establishing and enforcing standards. And while that effort emanated from a variety of leaders across the U.S. Air Force, the charge was led principally by General Wilbur "Bill" Creech who commanded Tactical Air Command from 1978 to 1984.

In *Every Man a Tiger*, Clancy does a thorough job chronicling General Creech's approach and influence in reshaping the Service. And Chuck Horner was one of an entire generation of leaders who learned and benefitted from their association with General Creech. Without trying to oversimplify what was a complex, multi-faceted approach to reinventing the Air Force, I believe the main credit should go to the reestablishment of a set of strong standards within the Service and assignment of responsibility for achieving those standards.

Prior to General Creech's elevation to command of Tactical Air Command, reporting accuracy of operational data was a huge issue. Unit readiness ratings were inflated. In the late 1970s an anonymous letter published in the *Air Force Times* challenged what had become the somewhat accepted practice of exaggerating bombing scores (read accounting principles) during training. What started as one letter grew into a groundswell within the service and raised the issue to prominence within the Air Force. The ensuing debate became pivotal in what was a painful but necessary reevaluation of our ethical standards and the need for leaders to take responsibility for the performance of their organizations. It didn't come easily, but it was becoming clear by the early 1980s that a profound and positive change was taking place.

Many attribute the improved performance of the Air Force and all the military services to the funding increased provided during the early years of the Reagan administration. But while those improvements and modernization were certainly needed, the change that was taking place preceded by a few years the effects of any budgetary improvements. General Creech retired from active duty in 1984, about the time that the Reagan budget increases were finally resulting in new equipment hitting the field. By then, the Air Force's transformation had already been in full swing for a number of years. That transformation was based on the reestablishment of performance standards for everything that we did, and then responsibility and accountability for achieving those standards. And in his wake, Bill Creech left a generation of Air Force leaders who had bought into his approach for transforming the Air Force, a generation that included people like Chuck Horner. It was a transformation built not on money for new equipment, but rather on leadership, standards of performance, and accountability. It was the Air Force that would fight and win Desert Storm and succeed in countless other operations throughout the 1990s and beyond. It was an Air Force that would reinvent itself multiple times during the intervening years, but one that never lost its focus on standards or accountability.

That brings me back to General Horner's words and its application to today's business world. As I reread those few words, I come back to the concept of taking responsibility when things go wrong, even when there may be viable excuses. That's a hard notion for some to grasp, especially in today's litigious society. "Why should I take responsibility when something isn't the direct result of my actions," many will ask. The answer is simple: Because it's your name that's on the door right above the placard that says "Commander" or "General Manager" or "CEO." If you don't think you're responsible for anything and everything that occurs on your watch, then you probably need to find employment elsewhere.

In the last few years, as much of our financial structure has come unglued, we've been exposed to a barrage of CEOs, CFOs and corporate officers in the public arena pronouncing their lack of culpability because they didn't know what was going on in their organization or some other technicality that supposedly made the problem someone else's responsibility. It's appalling to watch. Had our military services allowed that type of blame-it-on-someone-else mentality to take hold, we would not have accomplished the successes of Desert Storm and those that followed. Our military was fortunate to have leaders like Bill Creech, Chuck Horner and countless others who understood the concept of service and accountability at a time when strong leadership was needed most.

Some have suggested that the fix for the lack of accountability in certain parts of the business world is more regulation rather than a reexamination of the moral and ethical leadership that should exist in board rooms across America. While some debate the effectiveness of stronger regulatory mechanisms, I believe there is a problem with this approach that often gets lost in the discussion. Unfortunately, I think a drive for increased regulation sends the wrong signal to those just entering the business arena and even those who are already entrenched. It establishes the notion that right and wrong are determined by regulatory and statutory limits. Anything beyond that is considered fair game. That's a dangerous notion. And while it may not be a view that is shared or practiced by the majority of business leaders today, it is still far too prevalent.

I recall my own experiences in the 1970s as a young officer. And while my memory isn't what it once was, I still clearly recall the overall tone that was being set as we revitalized the leadership within the Air Force and reset our ethical compass. It wasn't so much about establishing more stringent regulations to govern conduct within the service, it was about retaking the ethical high ground in the way we conducted ourselves on a daily basis. Yes regulations were enforced, but the focus was on honesty and accountability rather than on defining what was technically permissible. The change that took place in the Air Force during the late '70s and '80s was not lost on young officers such as myself, nor was it lost on the enlisted force either. It was clear that we had turned a corner and that our transformation was not centered so much on the letter of the law as it was on its spirit and intent.

Now a person's moral compass is generally established at an early age and, thanks to family, friends, church, school, and other influences, I was fortunate to have a strong sense of right and wrong long before I entered the Air Force. But the manner in which an institution like the Air Force operates every day sets the boundaries for matters that may not be so clear. And even people who think they have that strong sense of right and wrong can find themselves pushing the line a bit if that's the way the institution functions. If fudging on readiness reporting factors or bombing accuracy seems to be generally accepted practice and commensurate with success in the organization, then can we really expect a young officer to try and toe the tight ethical line? So likewise, how can we expect young businessmen and women to conduct themselves by the highest standards of honesty, ethics and morals if the company is lacking in that regard?

That's what leadership is about. That's where a leader has to "be ready to stand up and take the criticism and all the anguish when things go wrong." That doesn't mean a lengthy discourse on why things were someone else's fault. If you're in charge, then be in charge and stand up and take the responsibility. And when things go right, give the credit to someone else. I've had the opportunity to observe many people in leadership positions over the years, and I've learned something from each and every observation both in the military and in the business world. The ones that are successful in the long run are those that understand the concept of responsibility and readily accept it even when things go wrong. I have encountered absolutely no exceptions to that rule. They are the ones worthy of the term "leader." The rest are just filling the office.

It is possible to conduct business in a highly ethical manner, even in today's marketplace. If one examines those companies that are the most highly respected in the business arena, I believe a clear pattern emerges. That pattern involves senior leaders that have a long business horizon, and who understand that the foundation of their success and the success of their team is predicated on a strong code of business ethics. Those are leaders who understand the concept of accountability and who demonstrate it even when the sledding is tough.

Profiles in Patriotic Leadership

BIOGRAPHY

Lieutenant General Donald J. Wetekam entered the Air Force in June 1973 after graduating from the U.S. Air Force Academy. A career logistics officer, Wetekam commanded three maintenance squadrons, a logistics group and a logistics center. He served staff tours at both major command and Air Staff levels. He holds a master maintenance badge, a basic parachutist rating, and is the only general officer in Air Force history qualified to wear the explosive ordnance disposal badge.

Upon retirement from the Air Force in 2007, Wetekam joined AAR Corporation, a publicly held aviation services company. Initially serving as a group vice president, he established the maintenance, repair and overhaul functions as a separate business unit growing it to the second largest independent MRO in North America. He currently serves as Senior Vice President for Government and Defense Business Development.

CHAPTER 8
EVERYTHING HAPPENS BECAUSE OF LEADERSHIP

"Example is not the main thing in influencing others. It is the only thing."

- Albert Schweitzer

Rear Admiral Rob Wray, U.S. Navy

Much has been written about leadership. The topic has been sliced and diced ten thousand ways. At last count, Amazon had approximately 60,000 books available on leadership. Explanations and descriptions range from the overly simple to the unduly complex to the overtly silly.

I have been in leadership positions for forty years. My personal leadership experiences have run the gamut from starting and running small businesses, to running a 10,000 person multi-billion-dollar world-wide enterprise, from coaching a little league team to skippering a cold and frightened sailboat crew across the dark Atlantic. I have led while under fire in Iraq, while operating nuclear reactors, while struggling to keep a private school solvent, while trying to elect congressional candidates, on ships at sea, in boardrooms ashore. I have led in family situations, in school/college situations, in social situations, in military situations, and in corporate situations.

Along the way, I've read a couple hundred books about leadership and earned an advanced degree on the topic. I've written a book on it, and I've lectured on leadership in academic, military, and commercial forums. In short, I've studied leadership extensively, and I've experienced it extensively, in a number of forms.

I've learned a couple of predicate issues along the way:

First, leadership matters. With the exception of natural disasters, everything in this world happens because of leadership. Even the response to natural disasters is wholly dependent on leadership. Your school, your neighborhood, your town, your state, our country, our planet—the life we lead is the sum of a thousand leadership decisions. And the leadership decisions of today will dictate the life we lead in the future. Some think that somehow events will plod along regardless of the decisions we make—that we would have won World War I without Pershing and Wilson, or that Apple would have been great without Steve Jobs. They are wrong. Those who pooh-pooh the effects of leadership on our lives are gravely mistaken.

Second, leadership can be known. Leadership is not some ethereal unknowable genie-in-a-bottle. It is both art and science, but the science predominates. We can study leadership, we can observe it, we can measure it, and we can predict outcomes. It involves human behavior, of course, but like all behavioral studies, it is knowable. It is not magic.

Third, leadership skills can be acquired. It is true that some leadership attributes are inborn. Statistically, tallness and intelligence (both nature, rather than nurture) correlate positively to greater leadership skills. But with those two exceptions, virtually all of leadership can be acquired. The character of a leader can be acquired: empathy, honesty, vision, emotional intelligence. Similarly, the skills of a leader can be acquired: planning, decision-making, analyzing, delegation and the ability to speak and write. 98% of leadership can be created, in a person who has the time and the will to do so.

Those three predicate assumptions set aside; I have found in my study and in my experience, that there are four essential components of the successful leader. Just as we have never observed a water molecule without the requisite atomic components, I have never observed successful leadership without these four essential ingredients.

Essential #1: An UNDERSTANDING of the Situation

No one can lead without a thorough understanding of the situation or environment, in which the leader and the led are placed. Pick any great leader, from sports to military to corporate to government, and you'll never find one who didn't spend years, or more often decades, in that environment, developing the understanding that would be essential when eventually placed in a position of leadership and influence.

Many argue that Jack Welch was the greatest corporate leader of the 20th century; what many ignore is that he spent 20 years in the trenches of General Electric, moving from job to job in different industry segments, slowly accreting the base of understanding that helped him to be the incredible corporate chieftain he became. Similarly, at the same time as Welch reigned supreme in the corporate world, General Colin Powell led the US Military as the Chairman of the Joint Chiefs of Staff. Like Welch, Powell's leadership role was based on his decades of previous experience and understanding gained in many different positions within the military. Both were exceptional men; both were exemplary leaders; both were intelligent and skilled and savvy;

both rose to the top position in pyramidal institutions comprised of hundreds of thousands of competitive members.

Had Welch and Powell traded roles, could they have been as successful? Absolutely not. Just as Welch could not have run the military without Powell's background, Powell could not have run GE without the experience base that Welch built. Certainly, had such a mythical swap in roles occurred, each could have been a figurehead, and probably could have survived in the job by relying on their immediate staff. But neither could have been the transformational leader and the success that they were.

We see this all the time, in areas far less disparate than corporate vs. military environments. Could a great football coach become a great baseball coach? Not that we've ever observed. In fact, the opposite is true; we all know circumstances in which a great college coach is unable to survive at the professional level, and vice versa. Same game, but different environments. Different sets of understandings required.

Understanding the environment—having a visceral, intuitive grasp of the core issues that determine success vs. failure, as well as the infinite number of subtleties and nuances that collectively determine larger outcomes—is the first essential attribute of leadership. Without it, no leader can succeed.

Essential #2: The VISION of What Needs to Happen

Leadership is about change. Typically, it doesn't take leadership to maintain the status quo; it takes leadership to *change* the status quo, to get from where we are to where we need to be. The leader, in the end, has a vision of what should be, and that "should be" is different from the "as is."

The supremely important questions: Where do we need to go? What do we need to be? Sometimes, we must ask, WHO do we need to be? That's where the leader comes in.

Call it vision, or call it a sense of strategic direction. Call it the ability to make big decisions. More precisely, vision is seeing what the future should be. Getting to that future requires a number of decisions, most of which have to be made correctly to result in successful outcome at the desired future state.

In the military, before operational planners lay out the steps in a campaign, the leader must define the "desired end state." This is a technical term, but it encompasses the same concept as vision. The military leader must describe, "What is the ultimate outcome we want, and how is it different from today?" In the Iraq-Kuwait desert war of 1991, General Norman Schwarzkopf's desired end state was the removal of Iraqi forces from Kuwait, and the destruction of their ability to re-take Kuwait, once removed. His goal was to "win the war", but that doesn't produce enough guidance to making planning and execution decisions—he had to describe what "winning the war" meant.

Desired end state doesn't apply only to military operations. A church undergoes a revival and renovation: what should it be at the end of that process, and why? A company is failing, and need to be saved: what should it become? "Profitable" isn't enough of any answer—what should be the end state that produces profitability? A team is last in its league, and wants to become a winner. What is the end-state, the goal, so team executives can make decisions to bring it to fruition? Does becoming a winner mean growing a farm-system to produce better players, or trading for faster players, or investing in a stadium, or bringing on more experienced and more expensive coaches?

The leader must make these big decisions, and many of the smaller ones. But big decisions, once made properly, will guide and inform smaller decisions. If the big ones are done right, the others will follow. Conversely, if the big decisions are wrong, or are not made at all, then no amount of adroit management and leadership at lower levels will suffice.

Note that the ability to choose a vision—the correct vision—is dependent on one's understanding of the environment. Jack Welch made three or four remarkably important decisions early in his tenure as CEO of GE. Among them, he decided that if a GE business couldn't be first or second in its respective industry, GE would shed that business and concentrate its efforts elsewhere. That "vision" and "decision" on Welch's part didn't appear out of the blue—it was based on his 20 years in the trenches.

But many at GE had similarly spent 20 years in the same trenches, and didn't come to the same vision until Welch led them there. An understanding of the environment is crucial, but it is separate from the ability to envision the correct future, and make the decisions necessary to implement that vision. Understanding the environment, and making the decision on the future vision of the organization within that environment, are two different things. Two different skills are required, and the great leaders—the Welch's, the Schwarzkopf's—have both.

Essential #3: The SKILLS and Attributes to Implement that Vision

Assume now that a leader is well steeped in the environment in which she is leading, and that she has laid out a vision of the desired future state of the organization. Now, a third essential ingredient is required: the myriad of skills, attributes, and habits by which her leadership is practiced on a day-to-day basis.

First let's discuss attributes, or characteristics of the leader. These are who the leader is. A good leader is honest. She is well-spoken. She is well-read. She is a master of her profession or field. She has empathy for others. She has emotional intelligence. She cares about her people.

Next are the leader's habits. Good leaders have developed habitual ways of living that help them maximize their effectiveness. A good leader works hard; she puts in the hours, and she makes each hour count. She is punctual. She keeps herself physically fit and healthy to accommodate the demands of leadership. She eats well and sleeps well. She reads often to stay current in her field. She knows when to make a decision, and how. She prioritizes her workday and those of her immediate subordinates. Good leaders can both multi-task and simultaneously focus on the task at hand.

Finally, good leaders have skills that they employ based on the situation. A good leader knows how to hire well and when and how to fire an employee. A good leader can delegate. Good leaders run meetings well. They know when to work democratically and when to make a unilateral decision. They know how to plan and how to manage projects. They can write well to convince others. They can speak well, to convince, to inspire, to cajole. They can strategically manage and strategically communicate.

Attributes, habits, skills. A good baseball player has certain attributes (height, speed, eyesight). He engages in habits that help him to maximize his contribution to the team (training, diet). He has many different skills (throwing, running, batting, stealing bases) that he employs at the appropriate time. It is the net contribution of these attributes, habits, and skills that distinguish the major league all-star from the farm-league wannabe. So it is with leaders.

Essential #4: The WILL to Persevere

As mentioned before, leadership is about change. And change is hard. Change can be unbelievably, illogically, unreasonably difficult. It usually requires making humans do something they weren't doing before, and oftentimes that something is something that they don't know how to do, or don't want to do. It means upsetting status quos, in personal relationships, in organizations, in processes. Virtually all institutions and organizations are designed precisely to institutionalize and protect the status quo.

What is the impetus for that change? What is the primal force that breaks down the barriers of resistance? In some cases, there is a collective sense of crisis which galvanizes non-actors into action. But more often, the prime mover is nothing more than the will of the leader. Even when the organization recognizes it is in crisis, many will be frozen in fear and will protect the status quo because it is what they know; it is a source of comfort and familiarity precisely when comfort is needed. Others in a crisis will be ready to act—the urgency will convince them of the need for change—but the direction of change will be unknown. An airline company is failing. What do we do? Sell airplanes? Cut payroll? Fly to fewer cities? Fly to more cities? Lower prices? Raise prices? Renegotiate union agreements? Maintain morale by refusing to renegotiate union agreements?

Whatever the vision—whatever the decisions—whatever level of adroit leadership and management skills is applied—there will be opposition. And the only antidote for opposition is the will of the leader.

And it can be tough. If you are reading this and have been in these situations, you'll know. If you haven't, you can't know the agonizing, excruciating effort required to overcome institutional inertia and intransigence. Imagine that you are the leader of a dozen campers on a shore of a river. You see that the forest on your side of the shore is on fire, and the blaze is moving toward you rapidly. There is only one thing to do—cross the river to get to the other bank. But many in your party oppose the idea. They say the fire might not arrive—it may start to rain—the river is dangerous—there may be fire or wild animals or other dangers on the other side. Imagine that you load them onto a raft, and you wade out into the river, personally pulling the raft by a rope. Imagine the dozen campers you lead sitting on the raft, with all their gear, complaining mightily, yelling that you're doing the wrong thing, and throwing rocks at you for having the impertinence to presume that you know where safety lies. Imagine that the river is made of molasses, and that you wear hip-waders full of cement, and the riverbed is slippery and rocky. Now imagine that it takes you weeks, or months, or even years, to pull your ungrateful flock to the desired end state that you know is the right place to be.

That's what leadership can feel like.

Imagine General Eisenhower trying to win the war by sitting in offices for years, for seven days a week, making thousands of phone calls, sending thousands of letters, trying to hold together a coalition of egos and martinets, all good people who had a hundred different views of whether and how to get to the other side of the river. Imagine President Wilson, who envisioned the United Nations thirty years before it became a reality, spending years trying to convince Congress and the country to ratify the League of Nations, and failing. Imagine Abraham Lincoln: half of his country was in armed conflict against him; half of the remaining half was the party in opposition; half of the remaining quarter was unsure if he was moving in the right direction. On a good day, Lincoln had 1 in 8 Americans on his side. Yet he persevered; he carried the union on his back, through the unspeakable trauma of the civil war.

In all change, no matter how self-evident, no matter how urgent, no matter how unutterably clear it is to you, there will be three factions. At best, one third of your group will be in favor. One third will be ambivalent—they may not actively oppose the change, but they will certainly not assist in it. And the last third will be opposed, and will actively fight it. The Newtonian force required to overcome the inertia of the ambivalent, and to counter the reactionary efforts of the opposed, is simple: it is the will of the leader.

In the summer of 1940 the world looked bleak to Great Britain. Hitler was on the march across Europe; France had fallen; British troops had been barely evacuated from the beaches of Dunkirk. The Battle of the Atlantic was long underway, and German U-Boats were sinking allied shipping so rapidly Britain was in danger of starving. The German air attacks—later called the Battle of Britain—had begun, in preparation for the inevitable German assault on England. To a population that had been so decimated in the World War twenty years previous, the obstacles seemed insurmountable. Some within the government advocated suing for peace and establishing a German-controlled government within Britain. Not Winston Churchill. In June of 1940, only a month after becoming Prime Minister, he addressed Parliament with his decision on the future of his country. Even though much of Europe had fallen, and more will fall, he said,

> We shall not flag or fail. We shall go on to the end. We shall... defend our island, whatever the cost shall be. We shall fight on the beaches, we shall fight on the landing grounds, we shall fight in the fields and on the streets,

> we shall fight in the hills; we shall never surrender.

At the crucial moment, at perhaps their darkest hour, Churchill provided the *vision* his country needed, but, far more important; he provided the *will* they needed to persevere along the difficult road to that vision.

Few humans will ever be called upon to supply the will to save a country, as Churchill did. But every effort, every change, requires human will to make it happen. Nothing that is important is easy. Every improvement, every step forward, requires a prime mover. That mover is the will of the leader.

Closing

Generally, a leader gains an understanding of the environment, then she chooses/decides upon a vision, then she uses all her leadership skills and attributes to bring about that vision. During that execution, she supplies the will necessary to propel the organization as it works toward that desired end state. While these four essential leadership components are exercised sequentially, they are not developed sequentially.

Leaders can develop capabilities in each of these four areas throughout their career. One starts small; one learns Understanding/Vision/Skills/Will running a 4 person business; one develops it and employs further at a 100-person business. Twenty years later, one would employ the same four essential components running a

100,000 person Fortune 500 Company. Although I have used examples of presidents and generals and corporate magnates in describing these components, they apply, and can be learned, at every level. They are universal.

Do not think that your situation is different. If you wish to be a leader, at any level,

- Thoroughly UNDERSTAND Your Situation and Environment

- Decide on the VISION—What Your Organization Must Do or Be

- Employ the SKILLS You Need to Effect that Vision

- Provide the WILL Your Organization Will Need to Persevere

The production of fire requires three different components: fuel, heat, and oxygen. No successful fire can be created without these three inviolable requirements. Conversely, a fire, once started, can be extinguished by removing any of the three. Similarly, the execution of successful leadership requires four inviolable ingredients: understanding, vision, skills, and will. With them, successful leadership occurs; take away any one, and leadership success dissolves. These four components are the bedrock upon which every effective leader builds his tenure. Disregard them at your peril. Embrace them—master them—and leadership success can be yours.

BIOGRAPHY

Rear Admiral Wray was born in New York, the son of a career Air Force pilot, and lived all over before entering the US Naval Academy. There, he was captain of the sailing team, Chairman of the Brigade Honor Committee, and graduated in 1979 with a degree in mechanical engineering. He served nine years as a Navy nuclear engineer including four years aboard USS *Mississippi* (CGN 40), completing several Mediterranean and North Atlantic deployments, including duty in Beirut during the 1983 Lebanon crisis. His subsequent reserve tours included USS *Fahrion* (FFG 22), Shore Intermediate Maintenance Facility Newport, Space and Naval Warfare Systems Command, 6th Fleet, and Readiness Command Northeast. Wray was then assigned as leading engineering officer at the aircraft carrier prototype reactors in Idaho Falls, Idaho. In November 1986 he transitioned to

Greg Slavonic

the Navy Reserve and spent the next twenty years in a variety of business leadership positions, ranging from technical startups to the hospitality business to regional manager for a Fortune 500 firm. During that time, he continued his Navy service, commanding five different reserve units and leading from 100 to 6,500 sailors. In 2004, he was mobilized to Baghdad, and led the startup of the first-ever operations center coordinating reconstruction of a war-torn country.

Promoted to admiral in 2007, Wray's first flag tour was as deputy commander, Military Sealift Command (MSC) leading 10,000 people, operating 180 ships in 24 time zones with a budget of about $3 billion. MSC operates worldwide providing fleet auxiliary ships, prepositioning assets, special missions, and worldwide sealift. In October 2010, he was promoted and assigned to Naples, Italy, as vice commander, U.S. Navy Forces Europe/Africa, and U.S. 6th fleet and now serves as President of the Board of Inspection and Survey.

He holds a Master's Degree from the McDonough School of Business in leadership from Georgetown University, and writes and speaks on the topic. He has written two books and holds a patent. At sea and ashore, in peace and war, in the military, in the business world, in his community, he has held a remarkable number of different leadership positions. His personal awards include the Legion of Merit Medal, the Bronze Star Medal, and the Defense Meritorious Service Medal.

CHAPTER 9

PAYING THE PRICE FOR LEADERSHIP

"All that is necessary for the triumph of evil is for good men to do nothing."

- Edmund Burke

Lieutenant Colonel Jim Zumwalt, U.S. Marine Corps (Retired)

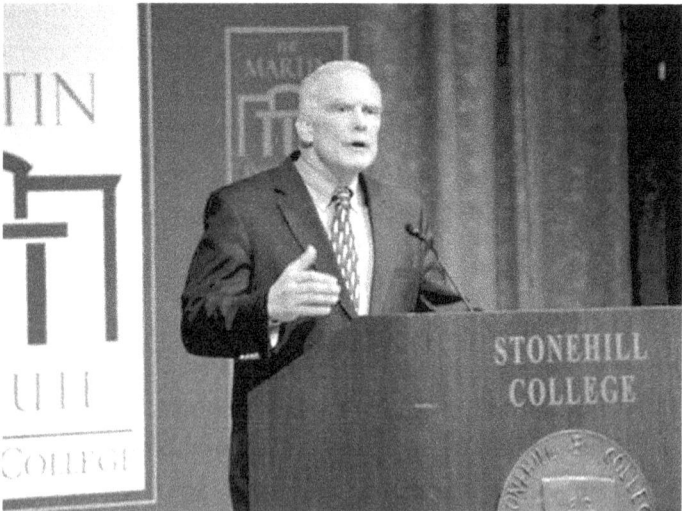

If ever a time arose during the 20th century in the history of the Free World when great leadership was needed to save it from a determined and evil enemy, it was World War II. As Adolf Hitler marched through

Europe and France fell, the German dictator looked across the English Channel to Britain. It would prove to be the leadership of one man, Prime Minister Winston Churchill, and his eloquence as a speaker that would empower his people with the courage and inspiration ultimately to defeat the German juggernaut.

But what if a leadership fiasco earlier in his career had led to Churchill being denied England's Prime Ministership during World War II?

Such a fate might have befallen Churchill, denying him his rightful place in history as a strategic leader during World War II, as decades earlier he had been a strategic leader in one of the most disastrous military campaigns of World War I.

As First Lord of the Admiralty in 1915, Churchill masterminded a plan to open up a new war front by launching an attack against the Dardanelles, controlled by Germany's ally, the Ottoman Empire. Known as the Gallipoli Campaign, it initially involved a naval attack. But when that failed, the effort turned into a ground campaign. For almost a year, British, French and Australian forces struggled to take the Dardanelles. Unable to do so, the campaign ended with a humiliating Allied withdrawal, over Churchill's objections. Costing the Allies more than 141,000 casualties, Gallipoli was considered one of the greatest victories by the Turks. The failed campaign led to Churchill's demotion— although he was not required to leave government service—and the collapse of Prime Minister H.H. Asquith's administration.

With the advantage of hindsight, many military historians give credit to Churchill for seeking to open up a second front against the Germans, thus forcing them to split their forces. Unfortunately, there were other factors that contributed to Gallipoli's failure.

Nearly a quarter century later, however, Churchill was able to recover from the ghost of Gallipoli to become a major strategist in the defeat of Germany and Japan during World War II.

By definition, a leader assumes calculated risks. Weighing those risks generate decisions by leaders impacting on the lives of those depending upon them to make the right ones. Churchill made decisions during the Gallipoli Campaign that came at a heavy price for those who carried out his orders. In modern times, great leaders never make such decisions with callous disregard for those having to implement them. It is the responsibility of the military leader to minimize the danger to subordinates by avoiding their exposure to unnecessary risks. It is the knowledge of this that motivates the subordinate to then dutifully carry out the orders given.

Sixty-seven years after World War II ended, courageous warriors wearing the US uniform are still being placed in harm's way. Having withdrawn from Iraq in 2011, US forces remain engaged in the longest military conflict in

American history. Today's battlefield is Afghanistan, but the concerns a leader has for unnecessarily exposing subordinates to risks are just as real today as they were in Churchill's time.

Unfortunately what is happening on today's battlefield is leaders recognizing a duty to subordinates to minimize risks to their subordinates and taking steps to do so are being victimized by a military system infected by a political correctness (PC) virus that is proving lethal to their careers.

It is against this backdrop this chapter details the factors at play in one leader's battlefield decision to meet his responsibility to his troops in minimizing their exposure to a deadly threat, which then subjected him to the PC virus. Understanding the factors at play in his situation and what caused him to act as he did should lead one to ponder, "What would I have done in his situation?"

* * *

It was August of 2008. Delta Company occupied Forward Operating Base (FOB) Airborne, located in Wardak Province, Afghanistan. During the first six months of a twelve month deployment, Delta Company was stretched thin, having to cover three additional outposts as well. It experienced a 33% casualty rate as the 90-man unit had suffered 28 wounded and two killed in action.

Delta seemed to be having a string of bad luck—or else the Taliban was just very lucky. The enemy seemed to know every move Delta Company made. It encountered ambush after ambush, mortar attack after mortar attack.

A classified division counter-intelligence report finally shed light on the reason for Delta's "bad luck." An investigation had determined Delta's assigned translator and several other locals stationed at the FOB—all of whom supposedly had been "vetted" by NATO forces—were communicating with the Taliban, providing them with intelligence on the company's daily activities. Twelve Afghans were identified in the report as being double agents. Delta's commanding officer, Captain Roger Hill, then 30, ordered they be disarmed and detained. Short on manpower as it was, Hill now had to commit additional soldiers to guard the detainees.

Their detention also presented him with another problem—a 96-hour clock to turn them over and officially charge the detainees. Due to the political fallout occurring after the Abu Ghraib Prison scandal in Iraq that came to light in 2004, the United States agreed, as a political favor to NATO allies who feared similar mistreatment by US forces in Afghanistan, the detaining unit had 96-hours after taking suspects into custody to formally charge them and turn them over to another unit.

This requirement was much more burdensome for US forces than it was for our NATO allies as the US had to deal with detainees more extensively than did they. The rule was impractical for several reasons—especially for isolated FOBs like Airborne short on manpower. It was an example of impractical PC invading battlefield reality. And, for the detainee to officially be charged, an investigation had first to be conducted by the detaining unit. This again tied up manpower and required a warrior to shift his focus from fighting to investigating. While well-trained as a fighter, he was not as an investigator, often even lacking the assets necessary to conduct a meaningful investigation.

Another issue was, in turning detainees over to Afghan authorities, they would only accept those accompanied with evidence of guilt, such as a confession. Therefore, U.S. forces were faced with conducting an investigation, obtaining evidence, transporting the detainees and then turning them over to Afghan authorities—all within the 96-hour period.

Detainees, on the other hand, knew how to play the 96-hour game. For those who knew they were guilty, there was no motivation for them to talk. By remaining silent, they bought time for themselves and, thus lacking evidence, US forces would then have to release them when time expired. The process basically became a revolving door for detainees, putting more than half of them back on the street and into circulation for the Taliban—just for having outlasted the clock.

The intelligence report sent to Captain Hill also had been routed to his battalion commander who, therefore, was well aware of Delta's detainee problem and the 96-hour requirement. Hill's unit made several calls to the battalion headquarters to discuss the situation and request support. The battalion was in the process of relocating to another province as their area of operation—Ghazni Province—had been deemed stable. Despite repeated requests, Hill's battalion failed to take custody of the detainees. Isolated at the FOB, Hill was left on his own to meet the 96-hour requirement. He knew failure to meet the deadline would release the "dirty dozen" to kill more Americans. (Interestingly, while the 96-hour rule was implemented in 2005, General David H. Patraeus, recognizing the rule's impracticality in meeting the four day requirement, petitioned NATO for additional time, recommending at least two weeks or longer. The rule was eventually changed in 2010 to a 14-day requirement with an extension beyond that time possible upon written request and at the commander's discretion.)

Since the intelligence report Hill received referenced a top secret source, he was prohibited from sharing it with Afghan authorities. This left Hill in a very difficult situation as, without being able to reveal the intelligence source, Afghan authorities would be unwilling to take custody of the detainees. The only way to beat the clock was for Hill to obtain a confession from the detainees, all of whom were determined to remain silent.

Time was running out. But the thought of releasing the dirty dozen, who had abused the friendship of their U.S. counterparts and resorted to treachery to inflict casualties upon them, did not set well with Hill. He knew their release would result in more Americans being targeted for death—including soldiers in his own company. Knowing the evidence in the classified report against the detainees was damning, he realized he somehow had to very quickly obtain a confession. Dire circumstances called for dire measures.

The dirty dozen were being kept isolated in a building at the FOB. Hill, along with a guard detail, went in and led three of them outside—lining them up out of sight of the remaining nine. Then, pointing his weapon at the ground, Hill fired three times. The nine remaining detainees were left inside to ponder the fate of the three outside. As Hill re-entered the building a short while later, confessions flowed freely. Delta was then able to transport the twelve to Afghan authorities and present them with signed confessions before time ran out.

Hill's actions that August day never endangered the lives of any of the twelve detainees. But, after failing to be responsive to Hill's numerous requests to accept custody of the detainees, not doing so and then leaving Hill in a leadership quandary, his battalion commander recommended an Article 32 investigation under the Uniform Code of Military Justice be conducted of Hill's actions to determine if detainee abuse had occurred. While Hill never directly threatened the detainees or had any intent to harm them, the charge stemmed from his actions in intentionally placing them in fear for their lives.

The PC dragon had reared its ugly head.

One of the reasons battlefield conduct for US forces is addressed under what is known as the rules of engagement (ROEs) is to emphasize to the enemy the US maintains a level of discipline that does not tolerate certain actions, such as prisoner abuse. The rationale of such ROEs is it thus encourages the enemy to meet a similar level of discipline in dealing with US soldiers in their custody. Therefore, the act of putting these detainees in fear for their lives, even if there was no intention to harm them, would sanction the enemy putting US captives in a similar state of fear.

Lost in the ROEs, however, is that we are now fighting an enemy with little regard for non-Muslim life. Only two months before the Delta Company incident, an IED and rocket-propelled grenade attack against three US humvees killed two soldiers outright. A third, badly wounded, was dragged out, and cut up into small pieces by the Taliban. The body was so badly mutilated that, when later located, it was at first believed to be the remains of two men.

About the same time, a convoy of fuel and refrigerator trucks was ambushed. As the latter vehicles looked more "foreign" to the attacker, the drivers in those vehicles were all beheaded.

There is tragic irony to think an enemy who believes his religion empowers him to treat non-Muslims with such brutality would be dissuaded from doing so by prohibiting US forces from doing as much as putting a prisoner in fear—if even not in actual danger—for his life. Clearly, what the US values as a strength on the battlefield, the enemy sees as a weakness. That irony was not lost on Captain Hill whose actions against the dirty dozen that day triggered the investigation—by the same command failing to assist him as he found himself in the precarious situation of having to choose between taking an unorthodox action to save US lives or not doing so, thereby putting those lives in danger.

This was not the first time a leader had opted in favor of the unorthodox action, triggering an Article 32 investigation and punishment.

In 2003, US Army Lieutenant Colonel Allen West was serving in Taji, Iraq as the battalion commander of a field artillery unit. An Army intelligence source informed him a civilian Iraqi policeman was plotting an ambush of West's unit. The Iraqi was taken into custody and, only after resisting arrest, was beaten by his guards. With little time to avoid the ambush, West placed his pistol near the Iraqi's head and fired a round into the ground. The Iraqi immediately gave details of the planned attack, later recanting as he claimed to have provided "meaningless information induced by fear and pain." While West later conceded he may have been wrong about the Iraqi's involvement, he said he based his decision on the intelligence he had received.

Nonetheless, West was charged and an Article 32 investigation was launched. He made no bones about his action and his intention in so acting stating, "I know the method I used was not right, but I wanted to take care of my soldiers." His actions won him the respect of numerous supporters, including 95 members of Congress who signed a letter to the Secretary of the Army in his defense. West was given an Article 15 proceeding rather than a court-martial, resulting in a $5000 fine and an Honorable Discharge. Such a discharge allowed him, unlike Captain Hill, to retain his full veteran benefits. He retired in 2004 and successfully ran for Congress as a Republican from Florida in 2010.

Interestingly, no further ambushes against US forces occurred in Taji during the remainder of West's tour there.

Unlike the support West received, Hill's Article 32 investigation made clear, once again, he was being abandoned by his senior leadership. Initially charging Hill with war crimes, the Army reduced those charges, ultimately finding him guilty of abuse for having put the detainees in a state of fear. Given the choice either to resign his commission or face a General Court Martial, which could require he serve jail time, Hill resigned. Under the terms of his resignation, he was also required to accept a General, rather than Honorable, Discharge— meaning he would be denied full veterans' benefits.

As the circumstances surrounding Hill's case have come to light, an effort has been mounted by numerous supporters to right an egregious wrong. Interestingly, among those supporting this effort is the Article 32 investigating officer, U.S. Army Col. Robert K. Byrd. In his post-investigation letter, Byrd notes, "Because the Division sealed the Article 32 results, missing from the larger view were the important matters of extenuation and mitigation, which were really never considered or publicized before the 101st Airborne Division levied punishments against CPT Hill or the other Soldiers."

Byrd's letter of support underscored several of these "important matters of extenuation and mitigation...never considered" in an effort to explain the difficult situation into which Hill had been thrust. Those matters, along with Byrd's recommendation, follow:

1. Delta Company had been assigned "an excessively difficult mission... for their experience level, the size of their unit and the size of Wardak. In fact... (the Deputy Commanding General for Operations for the 101st Airborne Division at the time) testified that during one of his command visits to the area, he recommended closing at least one of the Combat Outposts (COP) because he felt it was undermanned and under resourced. From this testimony, I concluded the detainee incident was partly the result of the Division and Brigade extending CPT Hill's unit beyond its capabilities. This was a direct result of what the Army commonly referred to as an 'economy of force

operation' when describing Afghanistan during this period."

2. Delta Company was "operating under a hostile and toxic command climate wherein any type of Battalion support was limited at best. Not only was there a personality conflict between CPT Hill and his Battalion Commander, Wardak never appeared to be the Battalion's priority of effort for support despite it being arguably the most difficult and dangerous area in the Battalion's area of responsibility. This resulted in CPT Hill... feeling isolated from their BN... (The Delta Company Executive Officer) testified about the lack of BN support regarding not only the detainee problem but in normal day to day logistical resupply and guidance... (This) testimony was supported by two other officers, who testified during the Article 32 (investigation)."

3. Captain Hill "testified concerning the impact the high number of unit Soldiers Wounded and Killed in Action had on the Company. He went on to describe an incident where he and his Soldiers sifted through the charred remains of an adjacent unit's Soldier after insurgents cut out his heart and cut off his arms so the insurgents could distribute the Soldier's fingers among local villagers."

4. Since the incident involving Captain Hill, "the 96 Hour Rule has since been proven arbitrary and without any concrete justification or necessity. It has since been abolished, as having been both ineffective and unnecessarily cumbersome; or, in a word, unworkable. Insofar as it was the perceived urgency of the 96 hour rule which caused these Soldiers to react the way they did to the insider threat posed by the Taliban agents discovered on their FOB, their cases should be re-adjudicated with strong consideration for these matters of extenuation and mitigation."

5. Accordingly, "matters of extenuation and mitigation along with the betrayal of a key interpreter facilitated CPT Hill... developing a sincere belief... (he was) alone in dealing with this problem. It was in this state of mind where the ends (protecting Soldiers) justified the means (interrogating detainees). As a result, CPT Hill... felt... (he) only had one chance to get the information... (he) needed to prevent additional loss of life."

6. Therefore, "I believe a full review and re-adjudication of this case to correct unjust, over reaching and inconsistent disciplinary actions against CPT Hill... is in order."

Byrd's post-investigation letter criticized Hill's command for both leaving him in a precarious situation and over-stretching Delta Company's capabilities, giving it a mission it would later take 20-plus times the manpower to perform. He also left no doubt that Hill always acted but with one focus in mind—to prevent additional casualties to a company already decimated by losses and an enemy's treachery. Just like Lieutenant Colonel West's motivation, Captain Hill's also to meet a leader's ultimate responsibility: "to take care of my soldiers."

Despite the strong endorsement from Colonel Byrd, testimony by other officers within the battalion that their commander was unwilling to assist Delta Company with its detainee problem and criticism of the battalion commander as being "morally bankrupt," Hill's appeal fell on deaf ears. His last resort now is to submit an appeal to the Board of Corrections for Military Records.

Concerning detainees, the ridiculous extremes of the 96-hour rule was evidenced by some suspects actually being given taxi money to get back home after having outlasted the clock. Another incident involved a militant actually caught in an ambush attempt who was wounded. He required hospitalization and, since the 96-hour period had expired by the time he received it, he was returned to the site of the ambush and left. Other incidents involve detainees serving on FOBs who are released and then able to report weaknesses in the FOB's defenses, later exploited in an attack.

Initially there was no way to track detainees once they were released. After maintaining a low profile for a while, they would re-emerge somewhere within the system. Hill's Afghan translator who was the ringleader of the group attempted to get reinstated at another FOB base several months later. But as a result of Hill's experience, a "no hire" list had been developed and maintained. When the new FOB commander could not believe the Afghan was a spy even though his name was on the list, the commander requested a waiver. It was denied and the commander was shown evidence of why.

Restricted by a questionable time regulation eventually deemed ill-advised for battlefield application, abandoned by a senior commander whose lack of leadership left Delta Company's Commanding Officer helplessly hanging, Hill did what he felt was right under the circumstances—giving priority to the safety of his men as did Lieutenant Colonel West five years earlier—and, unfairly, paying the price of leadership for having done so. As the enemy continues to brutalize US soldiers, other unit leaders such as Hill are being held to an idealistic battlefield standard of conduct. Out of Delta Company's incident alone, at least five of its members have been disciplined—some of whom were guilty only of being in close proximity but failing to report something "they should have known about." While they have been drummed out of the service for violating political correctness, the detainees involved continue to target Americans.

Article 32 investigations are seldom sealed, but require agreement by both sides to do so. As part of Hill's plea agreement, ironically making threats of imprisonment—thus using the same "fear factor" against him as Hill was charged with for using against his detainees—the Army pressured him to agree. It would appear that this was done for reasons linked more to preventing public discourse on the basis for the charges than for reasons related to anything else. If so, such actions by those involved represents a failure of leadership by attempting to cover-up the details of an incident in need of full disclosure, not only from the standpoint of gleaning lessons learned but ensuring fairness to those members of Delta Company who have suffered punishment as a result.

In 2006, a new book by Alvin Keenan entitled "*The Unknown Battle of Midway: The Destruction of the American Torpedo Squadrons noted* "every military triumph also contains tragedy." It details a series of faulty assessments of risks to subordinates and mistakes by military leaders that led to an 86% loss rate for one squadron and "the cover-up that concealed what actually happened." For Captain Hill and his men, they have endured the tragedy of what occurred; the final military triumph awaits a fair and impartial hearing of all the facts and the exoneration of these brave men.

The war in Afghanistan is being fought by less than one percent of the American population. It is being fought against an enemy more determined and evil than Hitler. We are blessed to have young men and women who courageously volunteer to go into harm's way to confront such an enemy. We demand incredible sacrifices from our warriors. But their willingness to volunteer and the sacrifices they make give rise to an expectancy command leadership will support them when a decision they make comes under attack—especially when the decision made is one erring on the side of saving American lives.

It is outrageous the military "system" did not come through for Hill. The fear he instilled in the detainees is no more than what anyone on either side of the battlefield encounters when the bullets start flying. Despite the fear the detainees felt by not knowing they were not being targeted for death, they were safer than on the battlefield where they would have been so targeted.

Hill deserved support from his command, but it failed him twice—once in the field and once in the military's judicial system. By his own actions, he demonstrated he valued his men's welfare above his own career; his commanders, by theirs, demonstrated just the opposite.

The 1979 Soviet invasion of Afghanistan proved disastrous for Moscow. One reason was it discouraged small unit leadership for fear it might one day turn on its master. The U.S. military, however, thrives on a leadership that never hesitates to take the initiative. But in abandoning Captain Hill, the U.S. military may be giving future warriors pause to do so.

There is a final consideration to be weighed by the military in its failure to support Hill's decision.

Winston Churchill's disastrous Gallipoli Campaign decision and the 141,000 Allied casualties that resulted was the consequence of a good leader rendering a rational judgment that, for other reasons, went horribly wrong. Captain Hill's decision and the lives it probably saved—a decision never endangering the lives of the detainees in his custody—was the consequence of a good leader rendering a rational judgment that went right. Had Churchill been drummed out of government service, the Free World would have been denied one of its greatest leaders at a time such leadership was most needed. How many future "Churchills" are being denied to us, at a time such leadership is badly needed, by allowing PC to trump a leader's difficult battlefield decision that ultimately results in lives being saved?

Knowing the members of Delta Company have yet to receive the justice they deserve, just ask yourself what would you have done?

Greg Slavonic

BIOGRAPHY

Lieutenant Colonel James Zumwalt is a retired Marine infantry officer who served in the Vietnam war, the 1989 intervention into Panama and Desert Storm. An internationally acclaimed author, speaker and business executive, he also currently heads a security consulting firm named after his father—Admiral Zumwalt & Consultants, Inc.

He writes extensively on foreign policy and defense issues, having written hundreds of articles for various newspapers, magazines and professional journals, including:

- *USA Today*
- *The Washington Post*
- *The New York Times*
- *The Washington Times*
- *The LA Times*
- *The Chicago Tribune*
- *The San Diego Union*
- *Parade* magazine
& others

Profiles in Patriotic Leadership

His articles have covered issues of major importance, oftentimes providing readers with unique perspectives that have never appeared elsewhere. This has resulted, on several occasions, in his work being cited by members of Congress and entered into the US Congressional Record.

His thoughtful perspectives earned him an invitation to join the prestigious Committee on the Present Danger (CPD), of which the honorary co-chairmen are Senator Joe Lieberman, Senator Jon Kyl, former Secretary of State George P. Schultz and former CIA Director R. James Woolsey. The CPD is a non-partisan organization with one goal—to stiffen American resolve to confront the challenge presented by terrorism and the ideologies that drive it.

Colonel Zumwalt is featured as one of 56 US military professionals in LEADING THE WAY, a book by best-selling author Al Santoli, which documents the most critical moments of the interviewees' combat experiences from Vietnam to Somalia.

He has also been cited in numerous other books and publications for unique insights based on his research on the Vietnam war, North Korea (a country he has visited ten times and about which he is able to share some very telling observations) and Desert Storm.

Colonel Zumwalt received a presidential appointment to be the Senior Advisor to the Assistant Secretary of State for Human Rights and Humanitarian Affairs, in which capacity he served from 1991-1992.

Because of his expertise, he also was asked to participate in a very unique educational project conducted at a high school in Raleigh, North Carolina, where he voluntarily contributes time and resources to educating students on issues of international importance.

He is author of "*Bare Feet, Iron Will -- Stories from the Other Side of Vietnam's Battlefields*" and "*Living the Juche Lie -- North Korea's Kim Dynasty.*"

www.AdducentInc.com
www.Adducent.Co

Nothing nourishes the soul like creating something.

That's what we do. We create, and help others to create.

Adducent is a publisher and creative company involved in book, screenplay and intellectual property development. We find, develop, write and publish stories with strong and positive messages that are entertaining, enlightening, informative and enjoyable to read. We also work with the entertainment industry to develop books and other intellectual property into live action and animated feature length movies and episodic entertainment.

- Publishing
- Publishing Assistance
- Writing & Ghostwriting
- Book, Story & Intellectual Property Development

www.ingramcontent.com/pod-product-compliance
Lightning Source LLC
Chambersburg PA
CBHW022336280326
41934CB00006B/656